THE LIGHTHORSEMEN

The Lighthorsemen. Copyright ©2017 by Jack Shakely.

All Rights Reserved. No part of this book may be used or reproduced, in any manner whatsoever, without the written permission of the Author and Publisher.

Printed in the United States of America.

Library of Congress Catalog Card Number: 2017958430
ISBN13: 978-1-932045-37-6
ISBN10: 1-932045-37-6
First Edition Paperback 2017

Cover Art from National Archives: Poster Advertising "Indian Territory That Garden of the World, Open for Homestead and Pre-Emption" in Current Day Oklahoma, from Records of U.S. Army Continental Commands, National Archives Identifier: 4662607; https://catalog.archives.gov/id/4662607

Strider Nolan Media, Inc.
6 Wyndham Way
Lancaster, PA 17601
www.stridernolanmedia.com

THE LIGHTHORSEMEN

A Novel

by
Jack Shakely

DEDICATION

To Jody.

DEDICATION

ACKNOWLEDGEMENTS

The Lighthorsemen completes my Creeks in Indian Territory trilogy.

The first book, *The Confederate War Bonnet*, begins in 1860 with an Indian Territory completely populated and controlled by the tribal governments of the Five Civilized Tribes: Cherokee, Chickasaw, Choctaw, Creek and Seminole. It ends with an ignominious defeat in a war far too fraught to be understood by those small unprepared nations.

The Lighthorsemen commences in 1895 when Indian Territory is clumsily, almost casually, being taken over by the white man. In only a few years, the Indian nations would be outlawed by Congress. But the Creek heart would continue to beat.

In the final book, *POWs at Chigger Lake*, which takes place in rural Oklahoma during World War II, the Creeks are more a secret society than a tribe, holding on to a language their children are forbidden to speak in school, and clinging to the customs of dance, games and burial that had served them for a thousand years.

Since the Unites States government re-established tribal sovereignty in 1971, the resurgent Muscogee/Creek Nation has regained its former strength, and now thrives with its own university, hospitals and shopping centers. Partly due, of course, to tribal gaming approved by the Unites States Supreme Court in 1991, the Muscogee/Creek Nation has shown itself to be a wise and prudent steward for its people. I am proud to be mixed-blood Muscogee/Creek.

My thanks go out to Dr. Judy Johnson, an Oklahoman of Choctaw descent born in Muskogee (the city and the nation spell the word differently). Her research, especially about the Dawes Commission, Indian headrights and the Osage Nation, was invaluable.

Thanks to Zach Weingart, the computer wizard who turned my shards of writing into a manuscript.

As has been the case in all three books of the trilogy, JoAnne Sanger has read every word, parsed every sentence and commented on every chapter the minute it rolled off my keyboard. Her carrot-and-stick (mostly carrot) readership propelled me through the dry patches.

My sincere thanks to my brilliant editor and publisher Michael Katz. An accomplished author in his own right, Michael untangled word snarls, threw light on dim passages and smoothed sentences, all the while maintaining my voice. He also designed the covers for all three novels. Thank you, Mike.

Jack Shakely
Rancho Mirage, California
September, 2017

BOOK ONE

BOOK ONE

CHAPTER ONE

In early August 1895, Billy Mingo was caught by the Creek Nation lighthorsemen, which is what the Creeks called their police force. It happened in a ravine behind his cabin near old Greenleaf Town, a long-forgotten cluster of villages now submerged under Lake Eufaula, Oklahoma.

When Mingo saw the lighthorsemen approach, he sprang up and ran a few yards. But then seeing he was outnumbered six to one, he just stopped, shrugged his shoulders in resignation, and turned to face his captors, most of whom he had known for years.

"You got me, boys," he said pleasantly. "But just for the record, if you weren't sitting them horses, I could outrun every one of you, and you know it, too. Well, every one, 'ceptin' maybe you, Clem," he added to appreciative chuckling.

"Where's your wife, Billy?" one of the lighthorsemen asked.

"I sent her and the kids over to her sister's in North Fork Town," Mingo said. "She started getting pretty scared, and I can't say as I blame her none. I went plum crazy with that damn homebrew choc there for a while." He had been walking back to the cabin where his horse, already blanketed, was waiting. He grabbed the hawser and swung easily onto the pony's back.

"I know what's coming to me, and I can't say I blame you none, either. But I do want to say there never was a man needed killing worse than that egg-sucking Tom Rains. Cousin or no cousin, I'm glad I did it." Mingo gave his pony a light tap. "Okay, boys, let's get on with it."

The lighthorsemen took him over to the Creek Supreme Courthouse in Okmulgee, where two days later the judges found him guilty and sentenced him to be shot to death.

In the Indian custom, the judges released Billy back to his family for a year, and told him to return on the first Saturday in August 1896 to be executed.

On the morning of August Fifth, quite a crowd gathered around the back of the courthouse where the execution was supposed to take place. One of those present was a young and impressionable college student named Edward Perryman.

Perryman was nineteen years old on that baked-ground, dusty August day. He had returned to Indian Territory that summer, after his first year of college in Fayetteville, and was now working the job press and setting type at his father's Okmulgee newspaper.

Perryman held tightly to a note pad and a pencil, pretending to be a reporter so he could get as close to the action as possible.

Two lighthorsemen rolled a wagon to a stop near the courthouse. They were joined by two other men who helped them remove bales of hay and set them up beside the wagon. One man took a stool out of the wagon and set it in front of the bales. Then, almost like they were responding to a silent signal, they took their places beside the stool, two on each side. Perryman was surprised how each man seemed to know just what to do.

Then the captain of the lighthorse came walking out of the courthouse and stood in front of the wagon.

"Is Billy Mingo here?" he asked the crowd. "You need to come on down, son."

There was a commotion in the back of the crowd, then the people parted.

"I'm here, Captain," said a man's strong voice, and Billy Mingo appeared. He paused to awkwardly put his rough hands on the heads of a teenage boy and a younger girl, a gesture as tender as it was obviously unfamiliar to the man. He then slowly and gently touched the face of his wife, trying to make his fingers remember her features, although he knew they would not have much time to remember anything. His wife and children stood dry-eyed, stone silent and motionless. Then he turned and walked to the stool.

Mingo sat down, tore his long white shirt so his chest was bared, put his arms down at his sides, and gazed up at the wispy clouds overhead.

One of the lighthorsemen said something to Billy that the rest of the crowd couldn't hear. Billy just smiled and nodded. Then the captain and another of the lighthorsemen positioned themselves in front of him, raised their rifles, and shot Billy Mingo through the heart. The roar of the gunfire seemed to make time go a little haywire. At first it looked like Billy just slowly rose off his stool. Then, faster, he flew backwards into the hay bales. The captain walked up and knelt beside him, then motioned to the men standing by the wagon. They quickly covered the body in a blanket and placed it in the wagon. There were a few murmurs from the crowd, and then it got real quiet again.

"Missus Mingo, I'll be bringing him round in a little while, if that's all right with you," the captain said. "All right, everybody. You all get on home now."

As Edward watched the wagon disappear behind the leafy oaks, he was shocked and humiliated to realize he was in tears. He dropped his head and started scribbling furiously in the notebook, afraid to show his emotions among the stoics. He was deeply moved, however, and the event would burn itself into his memory forever. He had just observed what he considered the most noble and manly gesture he had ever seen or even imagined. He knew then that he had no desire to work for a newspaper—or go back to college, for that matter. If even a murderer like Billy Mingo could show so much honor and respect for the law, Edward Perryman wanted to be a part of that law. He wanted to be a knight errant. He wanted to be a lighthorseman.

CHAPTER TWO

Looking back on that youthful decision, Edward realized that he had been motivated mostly by hope and bravado, with little understanding of the lighthorsemen's greatly diminished role as the century was coming to a close. It was a little like becoming a Knight of the Round Table after Arthur had been overthrown. Things were happening all over Indian Territory in those days that no Indian, much less a lighthorseman, could control. But no young man ever sees the big picture, and Edward was no exception.

He craved adventure, and the whiff of romance and danger was overpowering that hot summer day. He was going to be a lighthorseman, a courageous champion of the laws of the Creek Nation… just as soon as he screwed up enough courage to ask his father's permission.

Edward walked all over the Okmulgee hills, practicing his speech. He went down by the river, which was only a stream that time of year, and he silently reminded his father in absentia that not everybody was cut out for the college life. Then he waded across the creek into Green Corn Town, which only a month before had been a teeming mass of ribboned and festooned dancers at the annual Green Corn ceremonies. That day it was a stubbly, abandoned collection of picked-over cornfields and sagging lean-tos.

Perryman enjoyed the solitude and the lingering ghosts of tradition that Green Corn Town afforded. He stood before the sacred mound that was the center of the stomp ground, remembering and taking courage in the Creek heroes from distant times—great men like William Weatherford, the Red Eagle; Big Warrior; Little Prince; William McIntosh; and Opathle Yohola—and how strong and fearless he himself felt during those ceremonial days of the black drink and the Gun Dance.

Edward finally made his way over to Council Hill, which was three or four miles on the other side of town. He skirted the grassy old parade grounds of the long-deserted Civil War site Camp Kanard. There was a cluster of fellows playing ball, and they waved him over to join them, but he just waved back and kept walking. He didn't want to confront his father with a black eye or a throbbing head.

He made his way to the granary and stables, hoping to catch a glimpse of some lighthorsemen who he knew kept their horses there. And there they were, unharnessing the wagon that had recently carried the late Billy Mingo to the cemetery, talking and laughing just like the young gods Edward thought they were.

He ducked out of sight, squared his back, and started striding resolutely back to town, ready to face his father and the future.

His father was Benjamin Perryman. He was a full-blood, thrown as a child into the bloody confusion of the Civil War in

Indian Territory, a little-known corner of that conflict which pitted Indian against Indian and played out in the burnt and ruined cornfields of the Creek nation. Young Benjamin Perryman carried the mental scars of war, and although there was an old rifle in the house, he couldn't hit the side of a barn with it—nor did he give a damn. Pacifism wasn't a word used in Oklahoma in those days, but even though it didn't have a name, it had a home in the elder Perryman. Edward knew he would need to choose his words carefully.

As usual that time of afternoon, his father was sitting on the front porch swing with one of his ever-present little leather-bound books. He was wearing a pair of rimless glasses that Edward had long suspected were more a warning to be left at peace than an aid to reading.

As Edward approached the porch, his father looked up and peeled the glasses off. "Well, Edward, you've been out and about for some long time. I heard they executed Billy Mingo today. Did you see it?"

The young man appreciated the fact that his father always called him Edward, never Ed or Eddie. He'd done that even when Edward was just a tyke, which had made him feel grown up.

"Yes, sir, and it was amazing. He just came walking out of the crowd, sat down on a little stool and let the lighthorsemen shoot him. He never tried to talk them out of it, never said a word, just took his medicine like a man. I know it's crazy, but I think he even looked a little relieved."

"You know, he probably was. Come sit down, son," Benjamin Perryman said. He explained, "I've known Billy and his kinfolk for years, and he was a good man until he got liquored up. Then after he got sober, he'd usually feel remorse. That is why we always give condemned folks like Billy time to make things right with their family and neighbors—and most of all, I guess, with themselves. Billy's more at peace now, I think, than he would have been walking around with the blood of his clan on his hands."

"The lighthorsemen were magnificent, Father," Edward said, seeing his chance. "They were so respectful and honorable. It must be a very important thing to be a lighthorseman. I know you don't like guns, but I'm thinking that being a lighthorseman might be of some use to me if I want to enter the law."

Edward was being a bit presumptuous. He and his father had talked about him reading for the law, but they had also talked about the newspaper business, medicine, politics, just about everything except toe dancing. His father nodded and smiled.

"I am neither for nor against guns, Edward." He shrugged. "Guns are a fact of life. It would be like being against rain. But I *am* opposed to violence. And I have found that whenever guns are invited to dinner, violence usually takes a place at the table. I've seen it."

The conversation wasn't going as Edward had planned, but his curiosity got the best of him. "You've seen a gunfight, sir? What was it like?"

"Just its aftermath. You sure you want to hear this? All right." He stared down at the book in his lap, then looked up in remembrance. "It was the last year of the war, mostly just skirmishes, raids and robberies by then. We were living on that farm a few miles outside of Wetumka, and I was around eight years old. Although I didn't know it, a group of Stand Watie's poor woeful army tried to rob the bank in town and got ambushed for their troubles.

"I was in the chicken yard, below the house, when a man

came out of the trees, holding a rifle, running at me in a bent over trot. I could tell he was a rebel soldier, even though the only uniform he had on was that funny cap they used to wear. He grabbed me by the shirt and said, 'I am shot unto death! I am shot unto death!' I mostly remember his breath, which smelled like spoiled milk and something worse. 'Give a dying man some water, boy. Here, I'll trade you for my rifle.' He actually tried to laugh, but it just came out bloody coughs. Some of it got on me.

"I stood there like a statue, too scared to run. 'This is the chicken yard, sir,' I think I said. 'There is no water. Do you want me to run to the house?' 'Ah shit, ah shit'—you'll pardon my language, Edward—was all he would say. He grabbed the feeder and drank out of it, then ran back into the trees. Left his rifle behind. I don't know why, but I took it inside the hen house and propped it up against the wall; I guess thinking the dead man might come back and want it." He smiled ruefully. "It may still be there, for all I know. Your grandpa found his body about an hour later."

Edward wasn't about to be put off. "But the lighthorse are here to prevent violence, sir. I heard they brought Billy Mingo in without firing a shot. I might think you would be proud of a young man interested in keeping the peace."

"If we were having this conversation fifty years ago, my response would be enthusiastic. In some respects it still is, son. It wouldn't do us much good to write and enact the codes if we didn't have those brave men to enforce them." He looked down at the book still in his lap. "And I'm glad to hear you speak highly of them. I don't keep up with them on a regular basis, but I hear their ranks are a little thin these days. That damn Green Peach War ripped them up pretty good. When are we ever going to learn that as long as we keep fighting among ourselves, we don't need to worry about the enemy standing at the gate? And did you know that over in Muskogee they actually had two sets of lighthorsemen claiming to be the real ones? Just a bunch of finger-pointing, nobody got hurt, but a mess; so a lot more lighthorsemen just up and left. I didn't blame them. It's a shame."

"Then you would agree that the lighthorse need reinforcement?"

His father gave Edward a gaze so steady that the youth feared it might set his shirt on fire. Then he laughed gently. "Pretty good, son. Pretty good. You'll make a great politician someday. You took my praise and re-threaded it. Being a lighthorseman is important, although not as much as it used to be. There are some things you need to know before you make your decision."

Edward was almost too slow to catch the words "your decision" before his father continued. "This may still be called Indian Territory, but it's a white man's world now. It's a matter of jurisdiction. We are still trying to figure out how to work with the Cherokee, Chickasaw and Choctaw nations, and their courts and lighthorsemen. You know that a Cherokee can come down here and rustle our cattle or sell liquor, then hustle back across the border and our lighthorsemen can't touch him? Same thing goes both ways, I'm afraid. And don't think the outlaws don't know it, too. Some of those men like Dick Bass hide out down here when they're robbing the Cherokees, and hide out up there when they're robbing us. Then they rob us both and hightail it to No Man's Land, where nobody can get them.

"And then there's the federal government," Benjamin continued. "Now that the railroads are going through the Nation, they feel like they've got to protect the white folks, and I guess they do. So now we have Judge Parker over in Ft. Smith holding court. He's a tough old bird and only recognizes our lighthorsemen when it suits him. He put on hundreds of deputy marshals—some of them no more law-abiding than the men they are after—all over Indian Territory. Parker just sees our tribal territories as nothing more than lines on a map. And without putting too fine a point on it, let me just say that in a prisoner dispute, or even a dispute of fact, between a lighthorseman and a deputy, that deputy wins every time."

Benjamin Perryman put his hand on Edward's arm. "Last, Edward, and you may not like this: they are called the lighthorse*men*. You are only nineteen."

"Yes, sir; same age as Chief George Grayson was when he was a captain in the Confederate army and captured the 'J. R. Williams'. I mean no impertinence, sir."

"Yes, you are a natural-born politician," Edward's father said. He chuckled. "Well, you are a brave young man, and it's a young man's job. All right, I agree to your excursion into the law. But what do you say you try it for two years, then see how you feel?"

Edward brightened. "Thank you, sir. You won't be sorry."

They sat there on the porch as the evening crept in, the only sound coming from the katydids. After a few minutes, Edward's father spoke again. "Your mother would have been proud of you. And she would have asked you, as any mother would: can you take care of yourself out there? I hope you never have to use a weapon, but if it came to that, are you a good shot?"

Edward admitted, "Well, I've fired Mr. Landry's service revolver, but only a few times, so I need a little practice there. But I'm pretty good with a squirrel rifle, if I do say so. And you know I can ride."

"Oh, I never doubted you on a horse. You were born to ride,

just like me. And you may never have to shoot in anger. But just in case you do, I want you to be prepared. Come on inside with me."

Benjamin Perryman escorted Edward into the living room, opened the bottom drawer of the chifferobe, and removed a blanket-wrapped bundle. He unfolded the cloth to reveal a Colt Navy revolver. "It belonged to my father. It kept him safe during the war. I hope it does the same for you.

"When you go to Council Hill to join up, go see a man named Tom Sixkiller. He's a friend of mine and a captain of the lighthorsemen. I know he'll welcome you."

CHAPTER THREE

After more than fifty years in the saddle, Tom Sixkiller looked like he had been braided from leather. Sinewy and quick as a cat, his only concession to age was a shock of unruly white hair which looked like it had been styled with a hunting knife. On the day Edward approached him to become a lighthorseman, Tom Sixkiller was sixty-three years old—an age he never acknowledged. When asked, he would laugh and say he was 150 in Prairie Years.

Sixkiller knew every inch of Indian Territory, having walked and swam and ridden it since he was a restless teen. As a federal mounted soldier in the Civil War, he had chased Rebs up and down the Texas Road more times than he wanted to remember. He knew every hiding place in the Kiamichis, knew where to find water in the ancient cedar groves, and where to find small game among the rocks at Roman Nose. He could shoot the eye out of a turkey at fifty paces, catch catfish with his bare hands, and sleep in the saddle. Actually, legend had it that he never slept, a legend that Sixkiller did nothing to dispute and might have actually started.

He was a lighthorse legend, a mantle he wore with ease. He had been elected many times to serve as captain, an honor he gratefully accepted, but he refused to stand for chief, saying it would tie him down. Secretly, he was afraid of the paperwork that being chief entailed these days, because he had never learned to read or write.

Not words, at least. But he could read signs, marks on trees and moss, a bird sound or the absence of a bird sound, smells and tastes that would escape a lesser man. He had captured more than 200 men in his thirty years as a lighthorse captain, wounding a few and, when it came to that, killing some. He was like an animal in that regard, docile by nature, not controlled by anger or ambition, but able to tear a man to pieces without a second thought.

His men respected him immensely and feared him a little. He returned their respect with a fierce loyalty that was needed now more than ever. As the century petered out in the Territory, the lighthorse was in danger of becoming irrelevant.

Tom Sixkiller was tired and, for the first time in his life, confused. He understood being disliked, even hated; but not dismissed. At the Henderson Trade Store robbery the week before, the white deputy marshal got there first and actually shooed him off the porch. He knew that the old ways were dying out; hell, most of the young Creeks couldn't read or write their own language anymore. But he felt his people still needed him and the rules and tradition he and the lighthorsemen represented.

He didn't intend to leave this life in disgrace. He'd go with the same pride he carried as a young man. He wasn't looking for a fight exactly, but he'd been shooed away for the last damn time.

♦ ♦ ♦

A few days later, his affairs all in order, Edward saddled his horse and headed to the lighthorse headquarters to present himself to Captain Sixkiller to … join? Enlist? He didn't know the terminology. Sign up to be a lighthorseman.

He rode behind the stables and found an old schoolmate, Jubal Bull, sitting on the steps of a long building, drinking coffee and whittling. Edward said brightly, "*Hensci*, Jubal. I see you're protecting the bunkhouse from dangerous skulkers."

Jubal folded his buck knife and slid it into his pocket. "So that's what they call this place. I thought it was somewhere to stow your extra shirt and socks and to dream about while you sleep on the ground for weeks at a time." He smiled and stood up. "Edward Perryman, as I live and breathe. I haven't seen you in ages. Where you been?"

Edward dismounted and slung his reins over the hitching post as casually as he knew how. "I've been going to college over in Arkansas."

"Learn anything?"

"I learned I didn't want to go to college over in Arkansas."

"See there, you're getting smarter by the minute. Want some coffee?"

"I do, Jubal. Thank you. And I want a little information, if you would be so kind. Is Captain Sixkiller around? I want to present myself to him. It is about something else I learned: I want to become a lighthorseman like you."

Jubal slapped Edward on the back, which was about as deep a sign of affection as deemed proper between men in those days. "Damn, you really are getting smart. Although I doubt that you could ever aspire to be a lighthorseman quite like myself, we do have room for men of dubious skills like yours. I see you can sit a horse, which is half the battle right there. Come on inside."

They entered a long room with three bunks on each side. It reminded Edward of his dorm in college, only much cleaner. Beside each bed was a wooden peg, and half the beds had holsters hanging on the pegs next to them. Jubal noticed Edward's gaze go to them.

"That's how we take attendance. Holster on the peg means you are somewhere around here, doing chores or mending tack or something. We're in and out a lot. Have a seat."

They sat at a small field table against the far wall. Six tin mugs were hanging from hooks on the wall above it.

"Play your cards right and you might have a mug of your own someday, old buddy," Jubal said with a laugh. He pointed. "You can use that one there. I'll take you over to the coffee pot in a minute. It's next to the captain's office. But first there's some stuff you should know about life around here. Captain Tom don't say much, he mostly leaves that to me because he knows I enjoy it."

"I remember that from school."

Jubal laughed again. "Yeah, well, reading and writing was never my long suit. Anyway, here's the deal. Somehow or other, Captain Tom was told you might be coming over, and told me to be on the lookout for you because you'd be a goodun'." He gave Edward another playful punch. "Shows you how much he knows. So here's the important stuff. We get fifty dollars silver a month and take our meals over at Miss Robertson's boarding house. Let's see. Did I leave anything out? No, I think that covers it. Oh, except you don't get fifty dollars a month, you only get thirty. You only get to be an assistant lighthorseman until you get voted in."

"Voted in?" Edward scowled.

"Oh, hell, Edward, you know us. Indians are the votingest people in the world. We vote on our chiefs, we vote on our *miccos*, we vote on our lighthorsemen. Why, if you wanted to pass a law that night should always follow the day, we'd have to vote on it. And after everybody had their say, you might be surprised how close that vote could be. Yes, we stand every two years. You'll get your chance in the spring. But don't worry; if Captain Tom says you are good, you are good. Come on, let's go see him. I expect he's waiting for you."

They each grabbed a mug, and Jubal escorted Edward into a large room with a Franklin stove in the middle. Chairs were scattered here and there around two tables. One of the tables was covered in chalk dust from the tallies of a thousand domino games. Behind the stove, leaning against the door jamb of his office, arms folded, was a smiling Tom Sixkiller. Edward noticed that Sixkiller's relaxed stance still left him plenty of room to draw his revolver.

"Hello, Edward, and welcome. Your pa told me you might be swinging around this way. Hey, Jubal. I see you showed Edward where the cups are. Well, grab some coffee and come in, come in."

Sixkiller's small office was only slightly better furnished than the bunkhouse. Behind the desk was a framed railroad map of Indian Territory with red lines, dots and arrows added to it. To the right of the desk stood a limply hanging U.S. flag and a small bookcase. One of the shelves was half-filled with file folders. The other shelf held some law books and a Bible that Edward suspected was used more for swearing-in than spiritual enlightenment. There were no photographs on the walls.

Sixkiller sat in the swivel chair behind the desk and motioned with his hand. "Grab that chair and take a load off, son. It's good to see you." He held his hand out at shoulder height. "I've known Benjamin since we were like that. He tells me you are thinking of joining the lighthorsemen. I'd like that.

He's the very best of us, your father."

"Thank you, sir. He speaks most highly of you as well. But I'm surprised he already told you about my desire to become a lighthorseman; we only discussed it a few days ago."

"It's the Indian telegraph, Edward. You'll get used to it. Everybody knows where you are, what you're thinking, and what you had for breakfast." He laughed softly. "That's one of the ways we know somebody has pulled something: they clam up."

Captain Sixkiller leaned forward, put his elbows on his desk, and folded his hands in front of him. "Edward, I really have only one question for you. Why do you want to be one of us?"

Edward had expected this question and was ready. "Well, Captain, I'm thinking hard about reading for the law, and I figure what better way to see how the law works than to step inside it. Also, I have to admit I'm a little too restless for college at the present. But honestly, everything came together for me last week when I saw your lighthorsemen do their duty with Billy Mingo. The way that man and everybody else around him honored and respected our laws made me want to defend them."

"Are you sure there is no other reason?" He studied Edward carefully and added, "Revenge for your mother?"

Edward had not expected that, and rocked back in his chair. He looked down into his coffee mug. "No sir," he said quietly. "It's been more than five years now. Father says whoever did it is long gone or dead by this time. Father has gotten on with life and so have I. I do admit I still miss her, sir."

"She was a fine woman, Elizabeth. But the badge of a lighthorseman is not a bounty license." He paused. "Regardless of what some might say in Ft. Smith. Revenge lets loose the beast inside, the beast that will claw at your soul and hollow you out, sure as the world. It has no place here." He reached into his pocket and pulled out two silver dollars. "Enough preaching for one day. Here's an advance on your first pay. Go home and take your father out for steaks at the Calico and report back tomorrow morning. Now put your hand on this Bible and repeat after me...."

CHAPTER FOUR

In those sepia-toned moments just before dawn when dreams and thoughts get tangled, Edward felt an epiphany coming on.

Funny thing, Edward thought, how the truth can turn into a lie while it's still in your mouth. And how in his case the lie was really a much bigger truth begging to be heard.

Lying on his bunk and staring at the ceiling, the young man revisited his conversation with Tom Sixkiller about revenge for his mother's death. He had been only thirteen years old when she died, and the pain of loss stayed with him. Living with his father, who had set a stoic example, blunted Edward's grief and clouded his memory. Besides, there had been enough obstacles in his path to vengeance to daunt any man. When he was young, he didn't have access to a weapon, he wasn't a particularly good shot, nobody knew who did it, and even if he had found the man and somehow managed to kill him, he might wind up like Billy Mingo.

But even as he told Captain Tom that he had no interest in revenge, in that split second he realized that many of the obstacles would soon be removed. He had a gun now. Capturing bad men was what he was expected to do. And who knew? Maybe someday; maybe someday. Edward allowed himself a thin smile as he fantasized. He still wasn't much of a marksman, but that would take care of itself over time. And besides, how good a shot do you have to be to shoot a man point blank in the face? His smile broadened. Tom Sixkiller said that revenge would hollow him out. He sure didn't feel hollow. He felt the opposite.

Long suppressed fragmented memories, rumors and suppositions came tumbling back. His father, Benjamin, had been the smartest student at the Methodist Academy at Council Hill. In 1874, at the age of 19, he had been sent by the Academy to the University of Missouri, where he eventually attained his associate degree. During his time there he met Elizabeth Mason, who was a teaching assistant in Columbia. She was attracted to his smoldering dark eyes, and he to her quiet grace. Their son, Edward, seemed to have both characteristics.

On a morning in April 1888, Elizabeth Perryman had been out in the side yard hanging up clothes. Two drunkards, still half-crazy from the night before, came tearing down Okmulgee's main street on their horses, firing their guns and whooping. Elizabeth turned to see what the commotion was all about and caught a stray bullet in the chest, killing her instantly. Benjamin came home for lunch as usual and found his wife slumped over the clothes basket, a sheet still clenched in one hand. When Edward returned from school, his father stood on the porch and blocked his way.

"Doctor Price is inside with your mother, son. She's been in a bad accident, I'm afraid. We need to give the doctor room and stay out of his way." He put his arm around Edward's shoulder. "Let's take a walk down by the river."

Twice, as they walked the few hundred yards to the river, Edward pleaded with his father for some explanation. Benjamin

Perryman just raised his left hand in a command for silence. He never looked at his son.

They arrived at an old sycamore that had one massive limb jutting over the river. Benjamin stopped, turned his back to Edward, and leaned into the tree limb. He started talking into the sycamore, in a trembling voice that surprised and frightened his son. "Edward, I need your understanding now."

"What is it Father? What is it?"

"Edward, what I am about to tell you will change your life forever," Benjamin said, still avoiding his son's gaze. "Just as it will mine." He pushed away from the tree limb and took Edward's shoulders in both hands. There were tears in his eyes, which stunned the young man into silence.

"Your mother is dead, son. I am sorry beyond measure."

The older man's fingers dug deep into his son's shoulders, and Edward twisted away in disbelief and anger. "You're lying. You're lying!" he shouted. "She was fine this morning. She made pancakes. She wasn't sick. Can't the doctor give her anything?"

Edward's memory grew cloudy from that point. He remembered running to the house, which was now empty, then running to the newspaper, which was also empty, then just running, running, running.

Later it seemed the entire town was devoted to finding Elizabeth Perryman's killer. A posse was formed, over Tom Sixkiller's objection, and it took off in the direction they thought the drunkards had taken. They returned a day later, tired and, some at least, hung over. Without a single clue. The far more methodical and experienced lighthorsemen had also been tracking in earnest, but after four days, they too returned to Okmulgee empty-handed. They had picked up a trail, but it had headed into Cherokee Territory, and Sixkiller's men had no jurisdiction there.

It was rumored that the perpetrators were Dick Vann and that white man who rode with him, James Camp. But even though the elusive Vann was a bootlegger, robber, and killer all right, virtually every unsolved crime in the territory was ascribed to him, and there was no real reason to believe he was guilty.

But there was no reason to believe he wasn't, Edward thought. Dick Vann. Edward had seen his wanted poster on the lighthorse bulletin board, and thought he sincerely needed killing. In his morning fantasy, he thought maybe he'd been hasty in thinking he would shoot Vann in the face. Maybe he would shoot him in both legs and let him try to out-crawl the wolves back to town. Or, remembering a dime novel about the savages of the plains, why, maybe he wouldn't kill Vann at all, just cut off his fingers and thumbs so he could never shoot a gun again, or....

"Get out of bed, college boy," Jubal shouted. "What were you doing, dreaming of being a hero?" Edward's cheeks colored and he jumped to attention.

Jubal laughed. "Come on, assistant lighthorseman Edward Perryman, let's pack up our gear. We got word that they're bringing a wagonload of choc into Greenleaf Town tomorrow. It tastes like shit, but it will get you drunk all the same. You'll get to meet some of the fellows."

Edward and Jubal left Okmulgee just after daybreak. The leaves, grass, even the air seemed to breathe a mist. Edward loved watching the tendrils of morning fog and made the mistake of saying so aloud.

"Shee-it," Jubal said pleasantly. "What fun it will be to ride all over hell and yonder with a poet. Want we should stop and pick you some flowers?"

Edward enjoyed the joshing and had missed it. "The only flowers you are going to pick are the ones up your ass if you don't shut up."

"Really, Edward, such sweet talk may work with the college girls, but I'm iron-clad." Jubal turned serious. "Now's a good time to ask me any questions. Captain Tom can't hear us, so you can make them as dumb as you want."

"All right. Why are the lighthorsemen called the lighthorsemen?"

"Um, well … that is to say … I don't have a damn clue. See how educational this is? You are one lucky man, having me along." Jubal paused and grinned. "To tell the truth, at the risk of ruining my reputation as a Dumb Dora, I actually do know. We got named for a white man, of all things. Lighthorse Harry Lee was his name, and he had a famous mounted dragoon brigade that struck like lightning and won many battles. The Cherokees—at least the mixed-bloods—were picking up a lot of white man ways back in those days, and thought that would be a good name for their police. It stuck with the Choctaws and Chickasaws, too. We Creeks didn't have any trouble using the same white man word, lighthorse; we call ourselves Creeks, after all. Anyhow, pretty soon all five Territory nations had lighthorsemen. They proved a godsend during the removal."

"My father had a book about that," Edward said. "That's where I first read about the lighthorse. In fact, I thought they were started there."

"You might as well get used to saying *we*, old friend. You are us now and we'll make it official next month, if you still want to stand. Anyway, no, we didn't start there, but that's where we came of age. In the early days about all we did was round up strays and keep whiskey out of the towns. But during the removal there was so much to do just keeping people alive, and it was the first time all the lighthorsemen worked together, Choctaw and Creek, Cherokee and Chickasaw. It was a horrible time, of course, and thousands died. But thousands more were saved, thanks to the lighthorsemen."

"Is it true that white robbers attacked the people? What possible reason could they have had to turn their guns on those poor, starving women and children? It just makes my blood boil."

Jubal turned in his saddle to look Edward square on, and it was the first time Edward saw in the face of his childhood friend the fiery determination of an enforcer. "Well, it didn't take much to set a bunch of ignorant white men against us when that murderous rascal Andrew Jackson made it clear that he'd rather see every one of us dead than living in Alabama. They knew they could kill an Indian and never spend a day in jail. Besides, there was the rumor."

"What rumor?"

"It got passed along that when the tribes left for Indian Territory, our chiefs had been paid in cash money. Those white mongrels figured all they had to do was find the chiefs, kill them and take the money. Why, they'd have their own plantations in no time. And because they didn't know what a chief looked like, they figured they would kill us all first and sort us out later. But a lot of them didn't figure on the lighthorsemen. The boys did what they could."

"Aw, Jubal," Edward groaned, "I didn't know any of this. It's not in any of the books. How incredibly stupid: women and children standing naked in the snow dying of starvation while the chiefs were fat with money?"

"Rumors are stupid, Edward. Being stupid is what rumors do for a living. And as far as not reading about it in books, when was the last time you read a book about Indians that wasn't written by a white man? I guess if you want a book about us from an Indian point of view, you better write it yourself." He sat straight in the saddle and his face became that of a teenager again. He tugged at the brim of his hat. "Who gives a shit? Come on, I'll race you into town. Loser cleans the pots and pans."

CHAPTER FIVE

Edward won the horse race with surprising ease. In fact, when he entered town Jubal was nowhere to be seen and Edward was uncertain what to do as he waited. He wheeled his mount, looking for somebody who might be a lighthorseman.

Greenleaf Town, like all Indian towns, was more a haphazard cluster of structures than a platted town with streets. There was very little of what would become known as city planning. There would be a general store over here, a blacksmith and stable over there, a council house farther up the hill. If you wanted your house near a creek, you built it near a creek; if you wanted it facing south, you built it facing south. Charming, but confusing to outsiders, which might have been part of the idea.

Edward walked his sweating buckskin to the stable, where he came face to face with two men resting on their saddles, repairing tack. One was a full-blood with the traditional bowl-on-the-head haircut, long shirt, and moccasins. The other man, cutting holes in a rein with a Bowie knife, was wearing a derby cocked jauntily to one side. They looked up at the new arrival with absolutely no interest, then returned to their work.

Edward decided to take a chance. He hopped to the ground and, loosening his saddle, addressed the men over his left shoulder. "Excuse me, gentlemen. I'm looking to make contact with some lighthorsemen. Would you be they?"

The man with the derby laughed and pointed his knife at Edward. "See there, Chitto? It's the hat. He recognized the hat." He tapped his derby with his knife. "Yes, sir, you have found us, of course you have. Daniel Fixico of the sixth district lighthorsemen, better known as Derby Dan. That's what everybody calls me."

Jubal pulled his panting horse up next to Edward's mount and leaned forward in his saddle. "That's what absolutely nobody calls him, much to his displeasure. The man with the perpetual frown next to him is Chitto. Fellows, this here is Edward Perryman of Okmulgee, assistant lighthorseman and your newest stablemate."

"One of us?" Fixico raised his derby in a salute. "Fresh troops at last, Chitto. We're saved."

"You any kin to that newspaperman?" Chitto rasped. Like many Indians who spoke English as a second language, he seemed to be talking out of his back teeth.

"Benjamin Perryman, yes. He's my father, Mr. Chitto."

"Just Chitto. One name is plenty." He cocked his head toward his partner. "This fool is working on three. See what good it's doing him?" Chitto tossed a brush to Edward. "Here. Better brush him down good. Don't want to put a horse away wet."

Edward caught the brush and looked inquisitively at Jubal. "Put away our horses? I thought we were going to catch a bootlegger."

"Yeah, we'll rest up a bit here in the stable. Bootleggers deliver in the dead of night, so that's when we catch them."

Jubal handed his reins to Edward as he dismounted. Edward

joked to his friend, "What happened to you? I thought you might have gotten lost."

"Ah, you and that big buckskin were so damn far ahead, my pony and I decided to stop and relieve ourselves and wait for another day."

Jubal turned his attention to Fixico and Chitto. "Any news of our bootleggers, fellows? Did you talk to Old Man Chubco? He say anything about a delivery?"

"We asked him, sure, but he looked at us like we just shot his dog," Fixico said. "How could we possibly believe such a thing, he runs a clean store, as innocent as the day he was born, he wishes those choc wagons would just flat disappear, and so forth and so on. But Chitto and I saw his idiot son hightail it out of here about an hour ago, probably to warn somebody. So when we find the wagon, my guess is that it won't come as much of a surprise."

"It usually doesn't," Jubal said pleasantly. He explained to Edward, "There's only four of us, with more than fifty miles to cover. The bootleggers expect we'll catch them about once out of every five times ... which is probably about right. They just figure that in as part of the cost of doing business."

"Then why do we bother going after them?" Edward asked.

"Because selling spirits to Indians is against the law, and we are lawmen," Chitto said. "And sometimes it keeps people away from *micco homa*, old red king, and keeps them from doing something crazy like Billy Mingo done."

"Billy Mingo? Were you one of the lighthorsemen who captured him?"

"Yes, I was," Chitto said. "I stood right beside him when Captain Tom sent him into the next world. He was one of the ones we were talking about, weren't we, Funny Hat? He was a good bad man."

"I guess I don't understand," Edward said.

"Well, he killed his cousin—or at least the drunk inside him did—and Indians don't kill Indians and clan don't kill clan. He knew he done wrong, and he took his medicine like a man. Like a good bad man, that's what I say. But there was stories about that cousin of his: how he'd climb into bed with your woman when you weren't looking, maybe slap her around, too. Other people's livestock would show up on his land and he'd just have to kill them, so he said. He even sold a man a dead mule once, we got him for that one and made him give the money back. And here's the part we got talking about: this cousin, he was a damn *preacher*. He was one of those bad good men. You see them every day. Old Man Chubco who short-weights the widows and sings loudest in church; the Indian agent who accepts pork that's turned for the schoolchildren, while getting a side of beef for himself. Bad good men. They never seem to be in short supply. Why even that Judge Parker over at Fort Smith...."

Jubal interrupted. "That there is the mean to the bone men. Plenty of them, too. Don't get Captain Sixkiller on that subject or you'll get an earful. Come on boys, let's get something to eat and get some sleep. Edward, you are going to be too fidgety to sleep anyway, so you take the first watch. Wake me up at midnight."

Later, Edward sat on a hay bale, cleaning and re-cleaning his revolver, jumping at every creak and groan in the stable. Then he felt Jubal's eyes on him from where the latter lay on his bedroll.

"It's always a good idea to keep your piece ready, Edward, but I swear you are gonna clean that sumbitch to death. What's the matter? Isn't this what you signed up for?"

"I don't know. Yes, I guess so, but when I put a face to a

crime it gets muddy," Edward said. "I've been daydreaming about shooting bad guys for days, but when it comes right down to it … are we going to have to shoot anybody tonight? Are we going to come up on a good bad man or a bad good one, or a mean to the bone one? Walk me through this one please, Jubal."

Jubal spoke softly into the night, avoiding eye contact in order not to embarrass Edward. "If you are worried about getting shot—and I understand it's something to keep in mind in our line of work—you can breathe a sigh of relief. There will be no gunplay tonight; the stakes are too low. Too low on both sides. The bootlegger will be carrying a gun, but that's for robbers and wild animals, not for us. He knows if he shoots a lighthorseman, we will hunt him down and kill him. And if we don't, the Choctaw or Chickasaw lighthorsemen will. And if they don't, the Cherokee lighthorsemen will. The tribes are always fussing over territory and grazing rights and whatnot, but if you kill a lighthorseman—any lighthorseman—you might as well kill yourself while you're at it, because you are a dead man, sure as springtime."

"But what if he thinks we are robbers or wild animals?"

Jubal laughed. "Now don't go talking about Chitto like that. You'll hurt his feelings." Chitto grumbled something in Creek and rolled over.

"You will be amazed how noisy the night can be," Jubal said, lowering his voice even more. "Chitto is a fine tracker, but we won't need that tonight. Even a college boy like you, with one eye closed, could find a wagon-load of whiskey groaning behind a mule. We'll hear that wagon a hundred yards out. And when we do, I'll shout, 'Lighthorsemen. You are breaking Creek law,' or some such and it will all be over. Even the dumbest bootlegger in the world knows a mule and wagon can't outrun four men on horseback. The only ones who give us any lip are the white bootleggers, who are usually half-drunk themselves. They will cuss and moan and call us names, but down deep, they all just chalk it up to bad luck and make note to take a different route next time. We destroy the whiskey right in front of them, which is what we are told to do so temptation doesn't get to us, then we are all on our way."

The two men were quiet for a moment. "What about the Seminole?" Edward asked. "You didn't mention them. They have lighthorsemen, too, don't they?"

"They do, and they play a little rougher. They catch you once, they cut off your ear. They catch you again and, well, let's put it like this: of all the ways there are to die, I wouldn't put death by Seminole lighthorsemen as one of my favorites." He raised himself up from his bedroll. "They will kill you, but it may take a while, and your next of kin might not be too happy with what's left. Now get some sleep. I'll take next watch."

CHAPTER SIX

You could hear the creaking wagon, the ringing harness and wheezing mule halfway to Muskogee in the pre-dawn stillness. When they closed to fifty yards or so, perhaps out of boredom and wanting to change the pattern, Derby Dan Fixico began singing at the top of his lungs, "Oh, Mister Moonshine, Moonshine, better turn your tail. The lighthorse are on your trail." Edward thought he sounded surprisingly good, and joined in.

Chitto recognized the wagon driver. "Well, I'll be damned," he said. "*Hensci*, Tom Wilson, *hensci*."

"Hello, Chitto. You know I don't understand that Indian jabber," the man said. "Out a little late, ain't ya, to be running down innocent men. Go ahead, have a look and then let me be on my way. The wagon's empty."

Jubal leaned into the wagon. "Almost. But you didn't get rid of that dead man's breath stink of choc. Must of spilled quite a bit when you were stashing your whiskey. Must of been in a hurry. Your mule is all lathered up, too. Why, you'd think someone might have warned you we were coming." He looked in the direction the wagon had traveled and thought it over. "Where you been? Up at Robber's Roost?"

"Got no reason to be up that way," Wilson said. "And the fact is, this ain't even my wagon. I just found it when I was taking my nightly constitutional. Thought I'd take it back to Muskogee and try to find its rightful owner. Got to admit I smelled something funny, too. Maybe somebody was breaking the law, but it looks like they are long gone by now."

"You are about as good a liar as you were a lawman," Jubal said. "Edward, I'd like you to meet former assistant deputy federal marshal and current whoremonger, drunkard and whiskey runner, Tom Wilson. Sad to say, he has never been very good at any of those occupations."

"If I was a whiskey seller—and I ain't—I could make more money in a night than you do in a month," Wilson said.

Fixico grabbed the harness of the still-trembling mule. "You know, white man, you are just about to irk the hell out of me."

Wilson turned to Fixico and said, "Nice hat. Who'd you steal it off of?"

"Your sister at the whorehouse."

What followed was the longest five seconds of silence Edward had ever experienced. Then the whiskey peddler pushed his hat back and barked a fake laugh that missed by miles.

"Oh, no you don't," Wilson said. "You and your squaw man friends here know you can't arrest me, can't send me to jail, can't do shit because I'm a white man and naturally your superior. But get me angry enough to draw down and you'd shoot me, sure as the world. Well, not you," he told Fixico, "you are too slow and dumb-looking, but Chitto back there has his rifle trained on me even as I speak. Right, Chitto?"

"Something like that," came a growl from behind the wagon.

Wilson put both hands in the air. "Then leave me be. And

don't get any funny ideas. I ain't saying one way or the other, but smart money says Mister Chubco knows I'm out tonight and that you are sniffing around. If I should turn up dead, Judge Parker would have you hanged and buried before old Tom Sixkiller could get his boots on. Now let go of my mule."

Fixico tightened his grip. "I'm afraid I can't do that. You are right that our Creek laws can't touch you, but this here is a Creek mule. I can tell by its markings. And you said yourself that *you found it*. Well, this mule was illegally transporting spirits, and that's against our laws, so we got to take him in. Now you can come with him to Okmulgee and in a week, maybe less, we'll probably release him to work off his fine with some Creek farmer. Or you could start walking back to Muskogee and get there in time for breakfast."

"That's more than five miles, you black-hearted sons of bitches," Wilson yelled.

"Just right for a constitutional, I'm thinking," Jubal said pleasantly. "Come on boys, let's get this scofflaw mule to jail."

It took less than two hours to find the poorly-hidden stash of whiskey. With Chitto driving the wagon, the mule just retraced its steps. As the early morning light arrived, Edward could see that the wagon tracks led to a stand of cedar next to an outcropping of rock where, in the middle of nowhere, the tracks turned west for no apparent reason.

Behind one big cedar were some lumps covered by an old canvas. Edward laughed. "That has to be one of the worst jobs of hiding something that I ever saw. Might as well put a sign on it: free whiskey."

"Aw, I imagine that Wilson didn't figure anybody would

stumble on it before he got back in a few days, long after we were gone. That canvas is probably to keep it out of the weather and away from wild animals." Jubal chuckled. "Can you picture a bobcat drunk on choc? Scares me. Come on, give me a hand loading the stuff into the wagon."

"You're going to put it in the wagon?" Edward asked. "You told me that we destroy the whiskey on the spot."

"If we have the bootlegger, we do," said Dan Fixico, pulling the canvas away with a flourish like a magician with his cape. "*Ta-da*. We get four dollars for bringing in a whiskey seller, but if it's a white man, we have to let him go. But even if there's no bootlegger we get two dollars for bringing in the hooch, which Captain Tom dumps in the Deep Fork. Going to be some happy cattle downstream."

"They'll be partying with the drunk bobcats," Jubal said. He lifted a pony keg of rye into the wagon bed. "Plus this mule and rig will bring in even more money, all of which goes into the lighthorsemen general pot. See how easy it is to make money in the lighthorse, Edward? It's enough to keep Daniel in derbies, Chitto upstairs at the Calico, and after you stand for election, you'll get as much as we do. You can be up to your ass in books."

"What about you, Jubal?"

Jubal got a faraway look. "I save my pennies to buy some cattle and lease me a big old spread. Know right where it is, too. Down by Wewoka there's a valley covered in bluestem as high as your waist. Cattle get so fat on bluestem, you got to run them around a little every now and then or they're like to bust."

Jubal and Dan Fixico loaded three more kegs and tied them securely. Then Jubal clapped his hands. "All right, boys. Good night's work. Let's head back to Okmulgee and some hot food. Edward, you take the wagon. You are still an assistant lighthorseman for another week. So, what do you think? You still want to stand for election?"

"And be up to my ass in books? What could be better?"

When Creeks stood for election, they did precisely that. You declared your candidacy by informing the chief and standing at an appointed spot on the council ground. Secret ballots were unknown. People voted for you by lining up behind you. Some elections were close, but there was very little acrimony, except the occasional rift between full bloods and mixed bloods for first chief. The Creeks were a gentle people, however, trusting folks of the earth, and anything stronger than a barbed remark was unheard of.

On a crisp October morning, Edward took his place beside Tom Sixkiller, who was coming up for re-election himself. Edward was the only man running for the single lighthorseman slot, but it still filled him with pride when he saw his father take his place behind him. Benjamin just nodded and smiled and patiently waited for the counting.

When the counting was over, the crowd dispersed for a ballgame and barbeque. Benjamin lingered to shake Edward's hand, then put his arm around Edward's shoulder. "I'm proud of you, son. And ... I didn't want to pressure you one way or another into making your decision, but I think I may be in need of a lighthorseman, especially one with your skills. Walk with me back to the newspaper."

They entered the newspaper's front office. It was always clean, but also a bit dark due to the printer's ink dust that stuck to the walls and ceiling no matter how hard you scrubbed. The familiar smells of ink, newsprint and hot lead filled Edward's senses. He thought that after he was finished being a lighthorseman, he could always go back to newspapering.

Benjamin took the last week's paper from the rack on the wall and spread it open to pages two and three. He pointed to a column at the top of the third page. "You know I get paid a little by the federal government to record births, marriages, deaths and all property transactions in the area. This makes us the newspaper of record for Okfuskee district. Well, as I was setting type, something odd caught my eye, something that probably shouldn't have stuck, but did. I went back a few months and found what I was looking for. Then I decided to look up a few more names and, sure enough, there they were. What I found was no coincidence, son. What I found is very probably evidence of murder."

CHAPTER SEVEN

Benjamin poured his son a mug of coffee from the pot on the shop stove.

"Remember your old grade school teacher, Miss Boyd?"

"Little Old Lady Sadie?" said Edward as he blew across his mug. "Haven't thought about her in a long time. Why do you ask?"

"Well, she died some time back—and she wasn't really that old. She was only 45. She died of the grippe, which can carry you away at any age, I guess. But usually not that young; and usually in winter, not in the fall. Those are two of the things that got me thinking."

"Was she still teaching school?" Edward looked keenly at his father, hoping for a clue as to why he would bring his newly-minted lighthorseman son down to the newspaper to talk about a dead schoolteacher.

"No, and that is another thing. Sadie Boyd was a very smart woman, one of the smartest in these parts, and she understood the value of her headrights. Just after you went away to college, she exercised her allotment rights and got a quarter-section of sweet grazing land down near Wealaka. This made a lot of the full-bloods and pins angry, of course, because they think the land should stay in the tribe. But you and I know those days are over, and so did Sadie Boyd."

Benjamin lit his pipe and pulled on it in thought. "A lot of the townsfolk made fun of her after she took her land, saying she probably couldn't find it, much less work it. But like I said, Miss Boyd was smart, and she figured this out, too—or so I thought. Two months after she took over her place, I wrote up the notice that she had gotten married.

"Now this was surprising enough; as Jake Gardner down at the barber shop said, when God got around to Sadie Boyd, He gave her double portions of brains, but skimped on the pretty. And there was something else: Sadie Boyd married a white man named Theo Grady. I thought this was funny, and told the boys that we now had a Lady Sadie Grady. That is why the name stuck in my memory. I was having fun. I'm sorry to say, poking fun at Sadie Boyd became something of a sport there for a while; full-bloods were already annoyed that she had taken her headrights, and now men were making fun of her, a middle-aged spinster marrying a white man. Jake was especially tough, as I remember. He said, 'That Irishman married into a spread of blue stem and got himself a brood mare thrown into the bargain.' 'More like the old gray mare,' somebody else said, and everybody just laughed to beat the band. Little did we know she only had weeks to live."

Benjamin pulled some sheets of paper off a spindle and thumbed through them. "Next, among the notices Clem at the Indian office sends me every week, was this one. Stuck out like a sore thumb." He started reading. "'Change of ownership title of southeast quarter, section six, township 12, Okfuskee District from Sadie Boyd Grady, deceased, to Theodore Grady, husband.' Then down in the deaths column was a notice that Sadie had died the day before of the grippe and had been buried on the family homestead. I thought that it was downright disrespectful for a man to be making title transfers only a day after his wife died, and I went over to Clem's office to say so. Clem said, 'You ain't heard nothing yet. This morning a representative from the Missouri, Kansas and Texas Railroad came around with a bill of sales requesting another title transfer. Seems Mister Grady has been a busy man.' Turns out the railroad had bought 160 acres near Wealaka where the Katy line goes through. The railroad bought it from a white man, our very own Theodore Grady, for $200. Way below value. I smelled a rat, son, so I got on my horse and rode out to the Grady farmhouse. It was empty, and Theo Grady was long gone."

"Father, I'm confused. I thought a white man couldn't own property in Indian Territory."

"It's true enough that he can't *buy* property," Benjamin said. "But thanks to a very poorly-written section of the new Creek constitution, he can marry into it. The constitution says that Creek citizenship will be granted to any intermarried person irrespective of race or color. The provision was meant for the state Negroes married to freedmen, but it of course also applies to intermarried whites. So by marrying Miss Boyd, Grady became a Creek and could hold land. Can you see where I'm going here?"

"I do, and I hate it. Poor Miss Boyd. But Father ... I see how it could have *looked* like that white man killed her for her land, but couldn't it have just been a tragic accident? How could he have known about a few words in a Creek constitution that's still so new the ink is hardly dry? I certainly didn't."

"No, you didn't, and neither do ninety-nine percent of the people in the Territory—Indian or white. Not many people spend time reading our new constitution. But I'll tell you who read it backward and forward: the lawyers for the MKT railroad. Let's go see Tom Sixkiller."

♦ ♦ ♦

Captain Tom Sixkiller paced the large meeting room like a caged tiger, tapping his palm with a leather lanyard he used for a crop. Jubal and Chitto, knowing not to disturb the lawman in thought, sat quietly at the domino table.

"So, Ben, you are saying that the railroads are not only getting rid of us in general, now they are killing us in particular." It was a statement, not a question.

"That is how it looks."

"I knew ever since the Dawes Commission sent that army of surveyors out to plat those districts, townships, sections and I don't know what-all, they were actually measuring our coffins," Sixkiller said. "Now with the Indian Allotment Act and headrights forced upon us, they figured out a way to take away our land and give it back to us in pieces. They take away the corn crib and give us back a handful of kernels. 'Take care of these kernels,' they say. 'With real hard work and a little luck, they may be worth something someday. Of course, the railroad would be willing to take them off your hands if you'd like some easy money right now.' Bastards."

"I don't rightly understand why the railroads need land so bad they're ready to kill for it," Jubal said. "The Katy already has a strip of land from Fort Smith all the way down to Texas, and the Atlantic and Pacific is building up to Coffeeville as fast as they can go. I saw that with my own eyes in Vinita."

"Cattle," said Benjamin, a slight edge to his voice. "Instead of Texas cattle ranchers paying grazing fees to drive their stock to the railheads in Muskogee and Tulsa, why not hire some cowboys—white cowboys—to graze your livestock right here on your own land?"

"And from what I hear," Edward added. "Senator Dawes doesn't just want to take away the corn crib; he wants to burn it down. When I was in Arkansas last year, I read that Dawes had introduced legislation to do away with the five tribes completely. You can bet railroad money is behind that, too."

Sixkiller struck his lanyard against his leg so hard it sounded like a gunshot. "Bastards. But at least we can go down fighting. What are your thoughts, Ben?"

"Well, first, we should make sure this is actually happening the way we think, and not just our imagination. We need to go to the official newspapers in Wetumka, Eufala and Muskogee to check the marriage and death records of Creeks who married white men. If we are correct, poor Sadie Boyd won't be the only victim. As Mark Twain wrote, 'Once is an accident, twice is a coincidence, three times is a pattern.'"

"That's pretty good," Sixkiller said, cracking a smile. "See if your friend Mister Twain would be willing to be a light-horseman. We are always looking for men with brains. No offense, Jubal."

"None taken, Captain."

CHAPTER EIGHT

Tom Sixkiller sent Jubal back to the Boyd farmhouse to find the dead teacher and give her a proper Creek burial. He asked Chitto to hang around the Calico on the off chance that somebody might be throwing money around upstairs. Then he addressed Edward.

"Edward, you know your way around newspaper offices. Ride down to Muskogee first, and then over to Wetumka. Read through their newspapers to find if there are any more murders like your father suspects. And don't say anything about the possible railroad connection just yet." He turned and started walking back to his office, adding, "I'd go myself, but I cannot find my spectacles."

Benjamin chuckled quietly. "Edward, come on back to the newspaper with me first. I'll write you letters of introduction to both editors, they are friends of mine. I'll also tell them our suspicions, and what to be on the lookout for. They are probably not going to believe you at first; I almost didn't believe myself. But remember to look for patterns, Edward. And don't forget you are dealing with killers."

Edward didn't like going to Muskogee. Thanks to the railroad, in less than twenty years it had been transformed from a rambling Creek village into a rowdy island of hundreds of white men in a placid sea of Indians. It was the railhead for cattle, a massive trading company town for pelts of every description, and a jumping-off place for adventurers who were only vaguely aware they were in the Creek nation. It was illegal to sell whiskey to Indians, but because of the curious overlapping legal structures, white men could sell to other white men with impunity. The town was virtually an open saloon, and the Muskogee hotels (there were four of them) made being upstairs at the Calico look like spending time in a nunnery. The frustrated Creek lighthorsemen, who couldn't arrest a white man, had pretty much abandoned Muskogee, and the federal marshals only came to town when there was a killing or a rape. Given the burgeoning population of young drunk men with guns, both happened on a regular basis. Judge Parker even paid for a stable of deputized horses and grooms for the visiting marshals, who came into town on the same trains that carried the whiskey.

Yet, even though the Creeks in Muskogee were on "the road to disappearance"—as historian Angie Debo would write fifty years later—there were still hundreds of Indians in town. Some were flush with the false prosperity of Indian Civil War orphan payments finally arriving twenty years late and less than agreed upon, but in cash. And of course, there was the headrights issue that would soon turn Indian land ownership inside out.

Evidence of the latter hit Edward almost as soon as he arrived on the rutted and dusty main street. Two doors down from the *Indian Journal* office, and next door to the Union Agent, was a new small building with a plate glass façade. Written on the window in dignified gold letters befitting a bank were the words: Indian Territory Title and Trust. Below was the line: Acreage Bought and Sold. So it has begun, thought the young lighthorseman.

Edward entered a newspaper office that was almost a copy of his father's. Up front was a desk with an American flag, and a display case of inks, pens and stationery. The back held a job press, an array of small wooden boxes holding headline type, a Linotype machine, and a flat-bed press. There were stacks of newspapers here and there, and the smell of printer's ink and drying newsprint gave the entire place a faint swampy odor. When Edward was small, he thought that was the way fathers were supposed to smell. Now that he knew differently, it still comforted him.

"Can I help you, young fella?"

The editor of the *Indian Journal* was Victor Cox, a mixed-blood Cherokee who had learned the newspaper business in Tahlequah at the *Cherokee Advocate*. He was thin like Edward's father, but slight and a bit stooped. His thick glasses gave testimony to his many years of setting and reading type upside-down and backwards.

Edward handed Cox his father's letter like a foreign emissary presenting his credentials to the king. "Yes sir, Mister Cox. You probably don't remember me. I'm Edward Perryman, Benjamin Perryman's son."

The little man made a popping sound with his hand on his mouth, like a champagne cork leaving the bottle. "So you are, by God, the spitting image. I haven't seen you in … what? Five, six years?" He paused. "Bad thing, that. I am sorry for your loss. Well, you are a man in full now." He looked at the envelope and gave it a slight wave. "Has Benjamin sent you here to help me run this danged paper? I sure hope so. I could use somebody who knows his way around a printing press. When can you start? This afternoon too early?" He was joking, of course, but he kept his gaze steadily on Edward, on the off chance his wild guess had hit the target.

Edward bowed his head, then returned the man's gaze. "No,

sir. You honor me, but actually I have a job already. It's why I'm here. I am a lighthorseman, sir."

"Ah. Then you'd be working under Tom Sixkiller, huh? Well, I envy you, Edward Perryman. He's a legend. I thought about being a lighthorseman once myself, and I danged well might have, except for a few details like I can't see worth a damn, can't shoot worth a damn, can barely sit a horse and don't know north from south at night." He snorted another laugh, then stopped and studied Edward. "Being a lighthorseman is why you are here, you say? Just exactly what does that mean?"

"It's all in my father's letter to you, sir. We need your help. We believe murder is being committed, and the key might be in the official notices you publish in your newspaper."

"All right, son, all right," Cox said calmly. "Let's have a look. Pull up a stack of papers and make yourself at home."

Cox laid the letter flat on his desk and leaned over it with his thick glasses less than a foot away from the writing. Edward stayed quiet as the editor turned the pages slowly, went back to read the last pages again, then sat back in his roll-wheel chair. He cleaned his glasses with a handkerchief, reminding Edward of his own father's use of spectacles to gather his thoughts or command attention.

"Well, you and Benjamin have every reason to be repulsed by this treachery. I suppose in the cauldron of evil, there must be someone who reaches bottom first. This Grady fellow qualifies in my opinion."

"You believe it to be true, then?"

Cox took Benjamin's letter and shook the pages lightly. "To tell you the truth, the only real thing about your father's letter that surprises me is that it hasn't happened sooner—and it probably has. The Choctaws and Chickasaws have the same intermarriage provision in their constitutions, and the only reason I know that is because the Cherokee constitution doesn't. And that had to do with freedmen, not whites.

"But very soon it won't make any difference what our nations' constitutions say or don't say when it comes to land. When the surveys are finished and the Dawes rolls are finally drawn up, every adult Indian man and woman in the entire Territory will become the befuddled owner of a quarter section of land. There is not a damn thing our chiefs can say about it, either. It's the law of the United States, and most white Americans—if they think about it at all—are going to think that their country is being generous to us Indians, not pernicious. But we know better, don't we, Edward my boy? We know this is going to be like fishing in a barrel. Land speculators are going to be marrying and burying and cheating and stealing and wheeling and dealing until the white man owns every inch of this territory."

Cox stood up and took some newspaper pages off the spike. "That doesn't mean we shouldn't try to fight for justice for our people, does it? That's why you are a lighthorseman and, I guess, in a way is why Benjamin and I are newspapermen. 'Ye shall know the truth and the truth shall set you free.' That's the Book of Mathew, Edward." He coughed, embarrassed to reveal so much of his inner drive. His voice became gruff, and he started running his finger down one of the columns. "So what are we looking for? Names of Creek women who got married to white men? Then backtrack to find out if they exercised their headrights? Is that it?"

"Yes, sir," Edward said. "Then if we find one, I go out to the homestead and try to save the woman's life, if I'm not too late."

◆ ◆ ◆

After a frustrating and fruitless afternoon spent cross-checking headright title filings and weddings with Victor Cox, Edward gave up. He said solemnly, "To be honest, I'm glad we didn't find anything strange today. I don't know, maybe it was just a coincidence."

"Too logical to be a coincidence, Edward. Besides, it's all just a trickle today, but it will be a torrent soon enough. Thanks to you and Benjamin, I know what to look for. Go on now and get some rest. You staying with the Donaldsons tonight? If not, you are welcome at my place."

"I'm all set with the Donaldsons, Mister Cox, thank you." He stood and shook the older man's hand. "You've been very kind. I'll give my father your regards."

Caleb and Arlene Donaldson were the preacher and choir mistress of the First Methodist Church of Muskogee. Although outnumbered by the town's whorehouses, the Methodist and Baptist churches were making inroads into the Creek collective soul, especially when they sang hymns. Arlene brought a harmonium all the way from St. Louis, and the sound amazed and delighted the newly faithful. Many of the full-bloods in the congregation didn't understand all the English words to the hymns, but that didn't stop them from singing a rough approximation at the top of their lungs. Pastor Donaldson said it was indeed "a joyful noise unto the Lord."

Tom Sixkiller had made arrangements for his men to board at the parsonage whenever they were in town, avoiding the disreputable hotels. Mrs. Donaldson was a good cook and the preacher welcomed the addition to his meager income.

"We are happy to make your acquaintance, Edward," said

Pastor Donaldson in a voice that could easily reach the back pew. "We have been continually impressed over the years with how well-mannered all of Mister Sixkiller's policemen are. And you a college man, at that. Our home is yours. And we are both in luck this evening, because Mother has made navy bean soup and corn bread. Kings and maharajas could eat no better."

Later that night, they sat around the large dinner table enjoying sugar cookies and sweetened coffee. "So, Edward, can you talk about your mission?" asked the pastor. "Mother and I heard of some horses gone missing last month down by Emerson's store, but those horses are probably bought and sold three times by now. To be honest, we don't hear much. When you steal something, probably the last person you think to tell is your minister. So I just scold them on general principles." He laughed warmly.

"Well, Reverend, you probably wouldn't have heard of this crime, because it might not have happened yet. But if not, then it almost certainly will; if not here, then somewhere nearby." Edward went on to describe his hunt through the newspapers for the tragic combination of allotment, marriage to a white man, and sudden sickness that took Sadie Boyd's life. "I haven't found anything yet, but if I can see the pattern early enough I might be able to save another woman's life."

"What a cowardly act, Edward. I pray to God you find nothing. I must admit there are any number of white men new to this town willing to commit nefarious acts for pecuniary gains, even something as craven as that. Mother, you haven't heard of any such women taking their headrights, have you?"

"No, dear, of course not." She paused. "Though the lamentable story did remind me a bit of that poor Jimmy Bob Juniper."

"Oh, no, Mother, nothing of the sort. He was a man, and

besides the events didn't take place in the order Mister Perryman describes." He laughed again, but there was no humor in it. It was a signal that the conversation was over.

At the risk of offending, Edward pushed forward. "Can you tell me what happened to Mister Juniper?"

Pastor Donaldson held his open palm up to his wife with the unmistakable gesture that he, and he alone, would attend to the story. "Yes. Jimmy Bob Juniper died a few weeks back, but in some ways it is the exact opposite of the crime you are investigating. A couple of months ago, Jimmy Bob spent some time up in Coffeeville and came back with a bride. A young Irish girl named Molly; a bit on the plain side perhaps, but then, Jimmy Bob was a bit rough-looking himself. Besides, she came with other wifely charms. She had been a nurse back in the old country. He took his allotment, and they settled on a nice spread about five miles from here. He knew his cattle, Jimmy Bob did, and I think they might have made a go of it if he hadn't had the accident."

"Accident?" Edward leaned forward in his chair.

"Poor man got bucked off his horse and broke his neck. That little nurse got him into the wagon somehow and brought him into town all by herself. Doc Blanchard worked on him with Jimmy Bob's wife helping all the way, but he was too far gone. Sad story. But rather than kill somebody, that woman tried to save a life."

"Is she still here? I'd like to go out there tomorrow and talk with her," Edward said as casually as he could.

"No. She came to me and we prayed together. She was all upset. Said she didn't know a thing about ranching, and she couldn't stop thinking about Jimmy Bob. A fine woman. She said she was going to sell the place and go back to Kansas to work in a hospital or orphan asylum. Important work."

"She didn't happen to sell to the railroad company, did she?"

Pastor Donaldson raised his eyebrows in surprise. "In fact she did," he said, "but there's nothing unusual about that. The MKT is a ready buyer, and gave the poor woman a fair price."

Patterns, Edward thought. Patterns.

CHAPTER NINE

Dan Fixico hunched deeper into the blanket around his shoulders. It looked like his horse was being ridden by a pile of bedclothes topped by a derby.

"I think they ought to stop horse thieving in winter," he moaned. "They are going to sell their damned nags in Texas anyway, why not just keep on going till they get to San Antone or the Rio Grande, where they can eat oranges for Christmas and go swimming on New Year's? That's where I'm going one of these days ... Old Mexico with all them *senoritas* just begging to meet up with a cowboy. You ever been to Old Mexico, Edward?"

"I got as far as Fort Worth once and ate three bowls of chili, but that's about it. I read about Old Mexico, though. Sounds real pretty."

"I swear you are going to read yourself to death," Fixico said. "Guess that's why Tom Sixkiller had you going all over hell and yonder reading newspapers. Did you catch that low-crawling sumbitch who killed Miss Boyd?"

"Not yet," Edward said, "And it may not be just one man. It may be a whole gang of cutthroats. We've got every newspaperman in the Territory on the lookout, however, so it's only a matter of time." He squinted and pointed at a wagon in the distance. "Who's that, you think?"

The wagon approached the now-alert lighthorsemen at a slow walk. A big black man sat on the buckboard. He was bald, heavily mustachioed, and wearing a shiny silk vest that sparkled in the morning sun. Five men, four on one side and one on the other, walked, stumbled and trotted alongside. Their hands were tied and roped to the wagon.

"Well, I'll be damned. Edward, you are in for a real treat. That there is United States Deputy Marshal Bass Reeves, as I live and breathe. He's the best lawman anywhere. Maybe dresses a little fancy, but who am I to talk? He's a real nice fellow, so they say ... until he ain't." He put his pony into a trot, waving his derby in the air. "Hey, Marshal Reeves, it's me, Derby Dan Fixico. Remember? Creek lighthorse?"

The big man cocked his head to one side, then decided on tact over truthfulness. "Why sure ... Derby ... good to see you fellows again. You could give me some help, if either one of you can read?"

Fixico laughed. "You're in luck, Marshal. This here is Edward Perryman. He's been to college and everything."

"Well, then, I *am* in luck. Look here, Perryman, I'm too old to start lying now. I can't read worth a lick." He handed Edward a small stack of papers. "I got subpoenas for these murdering horse thieves, just as legal as you please. But these fellas," he pointed at the four men on one side, "are Cherokee, which means I got to deliver them to the courthouse at Tahlequah, and that fellow over there says he's white, so I got to deliver him to Fort Smith. And to tell the truth, I can't tell who is who and which is which."

"How did you even know they were horse thieves to begin with?" Fixico asked.

"Maybe I can't read, Derby, but I ain't stupid. I found a string of ponies hobbled outside their cabin, and when I made my entrance, they commenced shooting. I thought to myself, 'Yes sir, these men are probably guilty of something.'"

"There are seven subpoenas here," Edward said, "but only five men."

"Yes, well, that's why I need someone who reads to help me figure out who's who. I had to deliver two fellows to their Maker," Reeves said, chuckling. "There were so many bullets flying, I'm not sure if I got them or they shot each other. But they cheated me out of two bounties nevertheless."

Edward leafed through the subpoenas, then froze. "Which one of you is Dick Vann?"

"That would be me," said the man nearest the front of the wagon. "Want my autograph?"

Coldly, Edward said, "You killed my mother."

The man twitched and yelled, "I did no such a thing. That's a damn lie. Hell, I been down in Texas for nigh on to a year."

"It was six years ago in Okmulgee. You and another drunk were riding up and down Main Street shooting your guns like crazy men. My mother was hanging out laundry." Edward spoke in short bursts, trying desperately not to show any emotion. "You shot her. In the heart. She died. Instantly."

Dick Vann got suddenly pensive. "Is that what happened? I never did know. All I knew was that half the town was chasing me for days. And I mean days. And the lighthorsemen followed us all the way to Vinita—which, I might add," he drew himself full, "is located in Cherokee Territory, where your badges don't work."

"We must have missed the sign," Dan Fixico said. He looked at Edward. "Are you saying this is the man who murdered your mother?"

"I'm as sure as I'll ever be," said Edward, not exactly

answering the question.

Fixico edged his horse a little closer to the wagon. "Marshal Reeves, when you deliver Dick Vann to the Cherokee courts, they are going to hang him for rustling, correct?"

"That or a couple of bullets in the chest," Reeves said. "Dead is dead."

Fixico was enjoying himself. "'Dead is dead.' Hear the man, Ol' Dick Vann? Sounds like I'm singing 'Betsy from Pike,' don't it? But I'm a sporting man, and I got a sporting proposition."

He shifted his weight in the saddle so he could look at the marshal and Edward at the same time. His raised eyebrows were sending Edward a message, but Edward wasn't sure what it meant.

"Marshal Reeves, what if I was to tell you that Dick Vann here ain't a Cherokee, but a Creek? Would you release him in my custody?"

"As long as I get my fifty dollars' bounty, he's all yours, and welcome to him. He's been son of a bitching this and son of a bitching that ever since we left the cabin."

"Well. I ain't got it on me, but there's that much and plenty more back at the bunkhouse. Would you trust me ... us?"

Reeves thought it over. "Sure," he said. He stretched out his words. "I sure wouldn't want no jurisdiction disputes. He's all yours. You gonna take him to Okmulgee?"

"No, Marshal." He turned to the prisoner. "I got another idea. I'm going to let you go, Dick Vann."

Vann wailed like a bobcat. "You can't do that! Killed while escaping, you bastard? You can't kill a man in cold blood. You dirty son of a bitch, you'd drop me before I got to the end of the wagon."

Derby Dan turned stone serious. "Like I said, I'm a sporting man. I'm going to give you a chance, a chance you never gave Edward's mother. I'm going to give you a couple of hundred yards' head start, then I'm going to hand my Winchester to Edward. He'll be thinking about his dead mother as he takes aim, but, hell, who knows? Maybe the sun gets in his eyes, maybe a gust of wind comes up and messes with his aim, or maybe you make it to that stand of trees yonder where you duck and bob and tell your grandchildren how you outran the lighthorsemen. So stay here and be a dead man, or take off running and you got a sporting chance."

Vann seemed to nibble at the bait. "How do I know you will give me the head start?"

"We'll do it fair and square. When Bass Reeves thinks you are out a fair piece, he will fire his pistol in the air. That's when I suggest you start to gee and haw. Okay by you, Marshal?"

"Sounds all right to me." Reeves stepped down from the wagon and untied Vann's hands. "And you, Mister Son of a Bitch, are getting a hell of a lot better deal than I would have ever given you."

Vann didn't say another word. He sat down and took off his boots, then sprang forward like an animal. He was surprisingly fast.

Bass Reeves climbed back up on the buckboard to get a better view. The prisoners tied to the wagon yelled encouragement to the running man while Dan Fixico got off his horse and unsheathed his rifle ... all, it seemed to Edward, in slow motion. He felt that he had left his body and was observing the unfolding tableau from a perch a few feet above his head.

Dan handed his Winchester to Edward. "Here you go, buddy. Merry Christmas. It's a gift from your mother and me." As Edward dismounted and grasped the rifle, Dan said quietly, "It pulls a little left and up, so aim for his right buttock."

Edward took his stance with feet apart and knees flexed, just as Jubal had taught him. He pressed the stock firmly against his cheek bone to lessen any recoil, again as Jubal had shown, and waited. The sound of Reeves' pistol made him flinch, so he removed the rifle from his cheek for just a moment.

"Any time you are ready," came Bass Reeves' voice behind him.

Edward regained his stance and took dead aim. He thought for just a second how much the running, zigging and zagging Vann looked like a jackrabbit, his frightened and desperate path completely random. Then he noticed that one of Vann's socks had worked itself halfway down his foot, a pennant of hopelessness flapping here and there. On another day, it might have been funny.

"Take your shot," Fixico said. "Take your damn shot, lighthorseman. You ain't so good you can play him."

Edward pressed the rifle stock harder into his cheek. A few agonizing seconds later, he pulled the rifle down to a position known in the military as parade rest. Looking straight ahead at the disappearing prisoner, he said, "I can't do it. I don't know why."

But of course he knew exactly why. Since he was ten, people had been telling him how much he resembled his father. They walked the same, used the same hand gestures, some said they even laughed alike. It made sense that he would share his father's values, even some of the dormant and untested ones like an abhorrence of violence. Moreover, he thought that Dick Vann *probably* was his mother's killer, but how much did he really know and how much was teenage revenge fantasy?

"Give me that damn gun," Fixico said bitterly. He whirled and took a wild shot, but by that time Vann was well into the trees. "Son of a bitch!" He stomped over to his horse and threw the rifle back into its scabbard so violently, his horse shied.

"You going after him?" Bass Reeves asked.

Fixico walked his still-dancing horse to the wagon. "Nah, I got no authority. I might have been mistaken when I said he was Creek. But a promise is a promise. You'll get your bounty."

"Oh, don't worry about it. You can buy me a steak someday. I'll catch the black-hearted bastard soon enough. Men like him got to be criminals, just like I got to go catch them." He pointed his crop at Edward. "And when I do catch him, I want somebody at my side who is willing to use a gun, if it comes to it. That's all I'll say about that."

"I was thinking exactly the same thing," said Fixico.

CHAPTER TEN

Everett Pyle, attorney at law and general counsel to the Missouri, Kansas and Texas Rail Company, sat primly among the forest of potted palms that was the main lobby of Denver's Brown Palace Hotel. Across from him, drinking a schooner of beer, was a rough-hewn redheaded man in a jacket too small to button, with cuffs halfway to his elbows. He was sporting an auburn goatee that gave him a sinister whiff, like a frontier Guy Fawkes.

Pyle took a theatrical sip of his champagne. "I want to thank you for agreeing to come all the way to Denver to meet me, Mr. Macready. Thanks to you and a few others, my face is well known to every land office and Indian agent in the Territory. It wouldn't do to be seen together down there."

"No problem at all, Mr. Pyle. That MKT pass you sent me is better than Aladdin's magic carpet, and that's a fact. I just hop on in Muskogee and hop off in Tulsa—or Coffeeville or Baghdad, I suppose. It's a wonder, sir." Macready took a long swig of his beer. "And I'm about to make you even better-known. I'm about to put the finishing touches on another quarter-section. Only five miles from the Eufala railhead."

Pyle strummed the fingers of his left hand on the arm of his chair. "That's interesting, Mr. Macready; but as you know, there is an element of risk in these transactions, both for you and the railroad. And as helpful as you have been, the risks now outweigh the rewards. These are changing times, sir, and we need to change right along with them. That is why I have invited you here."

The redhead leaned forward and stage-whispered. "But I've got one just ready for the picking, Mr. Pyle. I need the money."

"You don't understand, Mr. Macready—nor should you. But it is heartening news I bear. When I said times are changing, I wasn't speaking metaphorically." Pyle was consciously using sophisticated language to establish his superiority. "My employers—along with those of the Atlantic and Pacific railroad and a bevy of factotums—have been prowling the halls of Washington to secure passage of the Curtis Act. It has cost us a fortune, but we have succeeded. Last month the Curtis General Allotment Act became law. Within months, our years of surveys and roll-taking will bear fruit and this great country will enjoy the harvest. The distribution of headright allotments will begin in earnest, land lying fallow will be put to productive use, many Indians will find themselves wealthy beyond their imagination, and America will be on the move again. Best of all for you, perhaps, is you won't have to sleep with squaws anymore."

Macready was confused, but tried to cover with bravado. "Oh, it ain't so bad. All cats are gray in the dark, as they say."

"Be that as it may," Pyle said impatiently, "in short order, all Indians will be free to buy and sell land to anyone, white or Indian, just like any other American." He paused and looked skyward. "In a way, one might feel sympathy for those savages. Imagine, Mr. Macready, being a fisherman and being told that the lake was being divided and parceled out. That's how the

Indians see the land, you know: a giant lake that isn't capable of being divided. They simply use it as their needs dictate. But even though they couldn't possibly know the word, their tribes are practicing Marxism, collective ownership that thwarts individual achievement and stifles commerce."

"Never heard of it," Macready said. Pyle refrained from smiling at Macready's faux pas, where Pyle had just demeaned Indians for not knowing of the concept.

"Well, it's been around for the last few decades—the concept, that is. It's a response to capitalism, I suppose. Ineffective, though. America has become the greatest nation in the world through the clearly superior economic theory of capitalism. Oklahoma and Indian Territory tribes will soon join our capitalist ranks, thanks to us." He paused again. "So, Mr. Macready, your services will no longer be needed." He handed his crimson-faced companion an envelope. "Now, don't rise to anger, sir. This money should provide sufficient balm to your nefarious deeds."

Macready grabbed the envelope and stood in rage. Pyle noticed that his pants were ill-fitting as well. He looked like the school bully who had out-grown his commencement suit. "Nefarious is it? I was doing *your* bidding. So I'm being given the sack, after I ... well, you know ... performed certain deeds for you and your precious railroad. I'll take your money, and I'll take my land as well." He shook his finger at the lawyer. "But let me just say this, bucko. I may have killed a few Indians, but you and your greedy railroad are killing them all, and that's God's truth."

Tom Sixkiller sat fuming at his desk while Edward and Dan

Fixico stood at attention in front of him.

"Just when I think you can't get any dumber, Dan, you prove to me you are a bottomless pit of stupid. Seven years a lighthorseman, and you pull a stunt like this. Stop looking at the floor. You are not going to find any forgiveness there. I should send you right back out there to find that cuss, but you and I both know I can't, the laws being what they are. So I'm going to assign you to Muskogee for a month. You can look for strays and cats in trees and break up barrels of whiskey while you ponder your future." He turned his flinty stare to Edward. "And you, well, you are anything but stupid, but you sure acted dumb."

"But Captain, I didn't even shoot my weapon. I didn't do anything," Edward pleaded.

"And that makes you feel pleased with yourself? You didn't shoot all right, but it wasn't because you chose not to; it was because you froze. You flat froze. You lowered yourself in the eyes of Bass Reeves, and if you think he's a good lawman, wait until you find out what a yarn spinner he is. How do you think I heard about it? Now look, Edward, I'm mad at you and that won't do either one of us any good, so I am going to suspend you for a week. Go home and spend some time with your father. You need to think if the lighthorse is the right choice for you."

"It ain't," Fixico muttered.

Edward sat on the porch swing with his father, watching the sun go down.

"I admit I've missed these evening talks together, son," Benjamin said. "The smell of wisteria, the first sprinkling of fireflies—the world and all of its parts seem to make more sense out here with you."

"My world is not making much sense to me now, Father."

Benjamin put his hand on his son's shoulder. He knew his son had been ruminating on the Dick Vann incident. "Yes, that has layers of complexities. For a lot of people, not just you. First, let me say how terribly sorry I am for never noticing the hurt you carried inside all these years after your mother's death. I should have noticed. We should have talked. Why don't men talk?"

Their protracted silence was all the more uncomfortable because it was now out in the open. At last Benjamin slapped Edward's shoulder and laughed. "See there? We're getting much better, I think."

Edward turned to Benjamin. "It isn't us I'm worried about, Father. It's the other lighthorsemen. I've disappointed Captain Sixkiller, Dan Fixico doesn't trust me, Chitto doesn't trust anybody, and Jubal? Well, he trusts everybody, but that doesn't mean I'm worthy of it." He quietly recounted the Dick Vann escape, leaving out nothing, one journalist to another.

"Crimes of omission carry heavy weight, it's true," Benjamin said. "And the weight often falls on others before it comes home to roost. But Edward, you unwittingly boxed yourself in. What if you *had* fired and killed him? Are you absolutely certain he murdered your mother? I'm not. And no offense, but Vann's death would have been reported as killed while attempting to escape. That would have made liars out of you and Fixico and, sorry to say, Bass Reeves, too. Sooner or later one of those prisoners could have exposed your lie; whether anybody would believe them is beside the point. You didn't shoot because of a moral fiber that runs through you wide as a river. You had a 'damned if you do, damned if you don't' decision to make and you chose humiliation over murder and mendacity. You made the best out of a devil's bargain, it seems to me."

"Then why do I feel like there's a hole in me? I couldn't shoot Vann, and it really wasn't the first time I flinched. Something inside of me feels broken, Father, like I'm living inside a lie. Three weeks ago, when we caught the Packer brothers robbing Keck's mercantile over in Wetumka? We snuck up on them with our guns out. Jubal shouted for them to come out peacefully. One of the brothers came roaring out the back door of the store, firing his pistol and turkey gobbling. "Fire," Jubal said, and I did, but late and high. Jubal got off a shot that winged the guy, and it was all over just that fast. But Jubal looked at me funny and said, 'Shee-ite, Edward, it's lucky Keck's has a roof, or you'd have plumb missed the whole building. Remind me to teach you how to aim.' He looked like he was laughing, but his eyes were asking questions. I couldn't return his gaze, and he saw that."

Benjamin played with his unlit pipe. "You may be forgetting that both of us saw your time as a lighthorseman as an experiment, not a life sentence. There are many satisfying careers—most of them actually—that don't require toting a gun. We both know you would make a good lawyer, son, with your powers of observation and persuasion. You got into the lighthorsemen only because of your interest in the law; it's just a rung in the ladder for you to climb. Well, the next rung will be reading to become a lawyer. And you know my friend, Judge John Whitten in Little Rock, will be pleased to have you read the law with him."

"It's hard for me to think about the next rung when I'm about to fall off this one," Edward said. "If the lighthorse is meant to be an experiment, sir—and I agree that it is—it is an experiment, in part, to test my mettle." He sighed. "How can I be expected to face up to Judge Parker if I can't face a drunk with a gun?"

Benjamin picked up his little leather-bound book. "Judge Parker isn't likely to shoot you; never mind the stories you may have heard. But I see your point. 'Screw your courage to the sticking place', as Lady Macbeth said."

CHAPTER ELEVEN

The lighthorse bunkhouse was quiet that April morning of 1897. Captain Sixkiller and Chitto, who often rode together, had joined up with Dan Fixico in Muskogee to hunt for the notorious Christian gang that had murdered the sheriff of Oklahoma City and was robbing and terrorizing its way east.

Edward sat cross-legged on his bunk, writing in his journal. Jubal sat backwards on a wooden chair and stared hard at a dime novel with an orange cover. The lurid cover art showed a frightened woman cringing in fear, her dress torn and the back of her hand to her mouth, as a Kiowa or some other Plains Indian stood above her brandishing a tomahawk. The book's title was *Seven Years a Squaw, or Savage Pirates of the Prairie*.

Jubal looked over at his partner. "Know what's funny, College? I remember reading real good when we were back in third or fourth grade, but I guess I'm out of practice. I remember a lot of the little words, but the big ones get tangled up." He pointed mid-way down a page and held it up to Edward. "What does this word mean?"

Edward put down his pencil and slipped off his bunk to look. "Tresses. That means a woman's hair. Usually, like here, it's used with another word like 'golden' or 'flowing.'"

"They got different words for a woman's hair than for a man's hair? I don't get it. Hair is hair, right?"

"Not to a writer. To a writer, even a dime novel writer, every word means something just a little bit different. To us, too, when you think about it. A fellow from New York might say a bird is a bird, but you and I know there's a big difference between a blue jay and a meadow lark. Same fellow says tree, and you ask, 'post oak or cottonwood?' Using the right words is like putting just the right amount of salt in a stew. Makes all the difference. Let me show you."

Edward took the book and started reading from the same page Jubal had been struggling with. "Listen here: 'Her golden tresses cascaded down her heaving bosom.' What do you think about that?"

Jubal frowned. "That's the part I was working on. What does it mean?"

Edward smiled. "Her long blond hair fell over her titties."

"Well, hell, now we're talking," Jubal said brightly. "That's what that says? Tell you what—you give me some reading and writing lessons and I'll teach you how to shoot straight. How does that sound?"

Before Edward could respond, he looked over Jubal's shoulder to see a boy of ten or so standing shyly at the bunkhouse door. "Yes, son. What is it?"

The boy's voice quavered. "You Captain Sixkiller?"

Jubal stood and walked toward the door. "He wishes. The captain's out of town. I'm Jubal Bull. I'm in charge till the captain gets back. What's the matter, boy?"

The boy rocked back and forth, trying to peek inside while maintaining an avenue for a quick getaway. "No trouble, Mister Lighthorseman, sir. I got a telegram is all, for Lighthorse Captain Sixkiller." His ten-year-old curiosity finally got the best of him. "Why do they call him that?"

"Because he didn't want to brag about the other three," Jubal said, and fished in his pocket. "Here's a penny. I'll trade you for the telegram. Now skedaddle."

"Yes, sir," yelled the boy and flew off the porch, his bare feet barely touching the ground.

Jubal handed the telegram to Edward. "Read it out loud, will you?"

It was from the editor of the Eufala *Indian Journal*. "Perryman pattern found. Saw devil in town. Believed armed. Woman in peril. Please send lighthorsemen. Danger. Ed McCurtain."

Edward lowered the telegram to look at Jubal. "Mister McCurtain is a good friend of my father and as solid as they come. I have to get over there."

Jubal became dead serious. "We go together, Edward. Maybe you forgot that I was the one who had to bury Miss Sadie. Besides, if there's one word I can read, it's 'danger.' Let's get saddled up. I'll tell Clem to get some boys to take care of the stable."

The two men pulled into Ed McCurtain's newspaper around noon. "I've been looking for the patterns your father told me about, Edward," McCurtain said, "because frankly I thought it might have happened here already. Middle-aged woman dying of an old age disease? And married to a white man? But of course, by the time we fit all the pieces of the puzzle together the poor woman is dead. So I hit on another thing to watch for. I started checking the court records for white men claiming Creek citizenship through the new constitution's provision for intermarriage. And there he was, big as life and twice as ugly: Thomas O'Malley, dragging his bride from one office to another, putting everything in his name. Poor little thing. Her name is Rainwater. Used to be married to that preacher who they say fell out of a pecan tree and broke his neck. Then she falls into O'Malley."

"So she's still alive?" Jubal asked.

"Far as I know," said McCurtain. "I know he hasn't sold the place to anybody yet, but as soon as he finally gets the paperwork all done, she'll be of no use to him anymore."

"So how do we do this?" Jubal asked. "If she isn't dead, our showing up might just light the fuse. But we can't stay there forever, neither. How are we going to be able to get her out?

"The paperwork isn't done yet, right?" said Edward. "That's our play. We'll say we're doing survey work for the Dawes Commission or something, and she needs to come into the Indian Office to sign some more papers. Can I borrow one of those binders and a pencil? I need to look the part."

McCurtain handed Edward a two-ring binder. "It sounds risky, but for the life of me, I can't think of anything better." He smiled. "Those are old entries for advertisements, but they look official, don't they? Bring back the binder, and good luck."

A half an hour later Edward and Jubal rode their horses up to a typical Creek "double cabin"—two small cabins, one for eating and one for sleeping, topped by a single roof, with a breezeway between them.

"You do the talking, Edward. Make yourself sound like a school teacher. I'll be right behind you."

Edward kept his voice raised but friendly. "Hello, Mister O'Malley, Missus O'Malley? May we approach? We have some important papers for Missus O'Malley to sign."

A beefy man with red hair exited from the sleeping cabin

into the breezeway. "What? What? This is not a good time. Who are you?"

Edward dismounted and stepped onto the rough-planked breezeway closer to the eating cabin. He held the notebook open before him like an ancient scripture. "We are Creek lighthorsemen, sir, working for the Dawes Commission in the area of recent allotments. It appears that, as a recent widow, your wife may be entitled to another 80 acres. If you and Missus O'Malley will accompany us back to town to the Indian Office, I think we can get this straightened out this very day."

The big man slumped against the wall of the cabin, placing his hand on his forehead in a way that reminded Edward of a dime novel cover. "Oh, me darlin', darlin' Nessie," he said in a voice that could be heard in the back row of any theater. "She entered into heaven these two days past." He produced a catch in his throat. "Oh, she was a strong one. She fought against that deathly demon with every breath she had. I mourn her passing deeply, as you can see."

The Irishman's histrionics were so blatantly bad, Edward feared it was only a matter of time before Jubal called the man out. Edward himself was struggling not to show any emotion. But as he moved along the wall of the eating cabin, he quietly drew his gun and held it under the notebook.

Jubal stood just off the breezeway in front of the horses. "So your wife was a strong one, is that it? Does that mean you had to put *two* bullets in her brain because one probably wasn't enough?"

"How dare you, sir. What are you accusing me of?" The big man moved toward the edge of the cabin door.

Jubal started to speak slower, more distinctly, as he always did in dangerous situations. "You have no way of knowing, but it was me who had to bury one of your last wives, Mister

O'Malley—or should I say *Grady*? She had a bullet between her eyes."

"You fockin' Redskin," the Irishman said and grabbed a rifle which had been leaning against the door frame.

"Don't shoot!" Edward shouted. "Don't!"

Surprised, the man swung his rifle toward Edward. But the breezeway was so narrow he couldn't get a shot off. To buy himself time he struck Edward hard in the shoulder and sent him stumbling backwards. This gave Jubal time to clear his holster. "You are under arrest for murder," he said, just as he had been trained to say by Captain Sixkiller.

The furious O'Malley turned his rifle back to Jubal, and Edward grasped that his own moment of destiny had arrived. He would not fail Jubal the way he failed with Dick Vann. He gripped his revolver and fired, aiming at the man's buttocks as Derby Dan had coached him. Then he fired again and again, and the man danced like a puppet. O'Malley was driven forward and slammed into Jubal until both went sprawling.

"I got him, Jubal! By God, I did. I killed that rat bastard." He paused his celebration and focused on a grisly reality. "Jubal?"

"Come help roll this fat sumbitch off me," Jubal said weakly. "I'm hurt, partner, hurt bad."

Edward pulled the dead Irishman away and immediately noticed a dark stain covering Jubal's stomach. "He shot you? I didn't think he had time to get a shot off. That son of a bitch."

Jubal tried to laugh, but it just brought pink bubbles to his mouth and a pain that made him wince. "Oh shit, Edward," he said, his voice shaky. "I can't move my legs. The bullet must have nicked my backbone while it scrambled my guts. Shit. I've seen this before. It ain't good, buddy. Lean me up against the wall, will you?"

Edward pulled Jubal to a sitting position in the breezeway. He moved the dead man's rifle, only to find it cold to the touch. "This rifle hasn't been fired." He paused. "Oh dear God, Jubal. Did I shoot you? Did I?"

Jubal moaned quietly. "Calm down, College, you couldn't help it. It's what they call a through shot. That murdering bastard Irishman was standing right in front of me." He smiled weakly. "He didn't even have the grace to hold on to the bullet that killed him. He had to pass it on to me." He grabbed his stomach and shook with pain.

"But you *are* going to be okay, right? There's a doctor in Eufala. Can you ride? I can help you, you can ride with me."

Jubal looked past Edward into the trees. "You know, I was born and raised in a cabin just like this one. It was on a creek over near Dustin. I remember asking my mother if we were named for that creek, and she said maybe, or one just like it. That made me feel proud. My gosh, it hurts, Edward. This is crazy. Leave it to me to die backwards—my legs can't feel nothing and my gut's on fire. No, I can't ride, but it don't make no difference. I sure hope they got a horse waiting for me on the other side. It's a cinch I won't be walking anywhere in the next world." He tried to laugh again, spat blood down his chest and started coughing.

"Don't talk, please. Just rest for a bit."

"Oh, hell, partner, talking's what I do best. Always has been. Listen, when you get back to the bunkhouse, there's some money in a sock under my pillow. I want you to have it. Dan would just spend it on fancy boots or something, and Chitto would spend it on women. I want you to use it to learn something besides cowboying. The territory needs lighthorsemen, but we need lawyers and newspapermen, too." He clutched his stomach and groaned again.

"I am so sorry," Edward said.

Jubal was looking back at the trees. "You know, I like it here. It was cold, but now it's warm. It don't hurt so much." He patted Edward's hand. "See you later, College," he said, and died.

Jubal Bull was buried on a hill outside of Okmulgee. In keeping with Creek custom, over a period of four days Jubal's friends and family took turns sitting beside the grave. While Chitto, Dan and Tom Sixkiller all put in their appearances, Edward did not leave his friend's graveside the entire time. Then once the fourth day was complete, he packed up his belongings, shook his father's hand, and pointed his horse toward Little Rock, his father's friend on the judiciary, and an uncertain future.

CHAPTER TWELVE

United States Marshall Bass Reeves was, according to his boss, "Hanging Judge" Isaac Parker, "one funny-looking duck." He had jug ears, a flowing handlebar mustache, which was rare for a black man (Reeves preferred the term "freedman"), bushy eyebrows, and a clean-shaven head. "They ain't gonna scalp this old boy," he would say, then roar with laughter. He was a legendary lawman, but also a raconteur who loved whiskey, cigars, fancy neckwear, and spinning yarns—many of which were true. He was, in today's parlance, "good copy." Newspaper and magazine reporters never came away disappointed, and he wasn't shy, especially if a camera was in sight.

In September of 1897, Reeves was holding court in the dining room of the Oriental Gardens Hotel in Ft. Smith. It was still very warm—a so-called Indian summer—but one would never know it by looking at Reeves' starched collar, light wool suit, and a large colorful bow tie that bordered on the outlandish. A half-empty bottle of brandy sat between him and the smiling and scribbling reporter for the *Police Gazette*.

"Your exploits and those of your fellow marshals are, I must say, incredible," said the reporter, choosing his words carefully. "But ... might you have some other stories, stories of lawmen who might not have toed the mark? Stories that my readers may find amusing or cautionary?"

Reeves took a belt of his pre-lunch brandy. "Oh, hell yes. Well, not so much about us U.S. Marshals. We live by the gun. We're tough customers. We have to be. We're knee-deep in desperadoes, and hand-picked to do our jobs. But that ain't the case with the Indians."

"What do you mean?"

"Well, each of the tribes has their own police force, what they call lighthorsemen. They don't do much, mostly, just round up stray cattle, catch a horse thief every now and then, and chase bootleggers off their land. It's against the law for an Indian to drink whiskey, you know." He laughed and savored another sip of brandy. "Maybe that's part of the problem, I don't know."

The reporter's eyes widened just thinking about it. "Are these real Indian policemen, with bows and arrows and hatchets and things? Now *that's* a story."

"Whoa, partner. Don't go getting ahead of yourself. Most of those Cherokees and what-have-yous wouldn't know how to nock an arrow any better than you do. They all have guns. But having a gun and using a gun are two different things, as I saw with my very own eyes."

"What do you mean, Mister Reeves?"

"Well, the problem with those fellers starts with how they get their jobs. They don't get hired, they get elected, for great Godamighty's sakes. Now some of them, like this old Creek named Tom Sixkiller, are damned good. I'd be proud to ride with him. But some of them maybe can't think of anything else to do, I guess, so they go stand in the middle of the street come election day, and if enough people vote for them then, whoomp, they're a lighthorseman. They don't have to know nothin' about the job."

The *Police Gazette* reporter laughed. "Some say the same thing goes for presidents and congressmen. Mind if I have a sip?"

"Help yourself. So anyway, one day I come across these two Creek lighthorsemen. I'm bringing back a passel of prisoners I caught stealing horses. I didn't have my glasses with me, so I asked them if they'd read my summonses and fit the man with the paper, so to speak. This one lighthorse fellow, the one doing the reading, he says wait a minute, one of them prisoners is Creek and therefore I ought to hand him over to a Creek judge. I say sure, glad to be rid of him, and I untie him from the wagon. Well, next thing I know, these two Indians are yammering back and forth about whether to bring him in for hanging or kill him on the spot. The short one—the guy wore a funny-looking hat—he says something like 'he killed your mother, you gotta pay him back' or something. With all that shouting and bickering, everybody kind of loses track of the prisoner. He figures he just as soon be hanged for a goat as a sheep, and he takes off running. The short one looks up and says 'Now you got your chance. Shot while trying to escape.' He pulls a rifle out of his scabbard, hands it to the taller one and says 'Do your duty."

"Where were you all that time?" the reporter asked.

"I was standing in the wagon watching my other prisoners. I couldn't do a damn thing. Once those lighthorsemen took over the prisoner, I lost what they call jurisdiction. That's a big thing around here. Anyway, here's this prisoner hot-footing it toward a stand of scrub oak while the Indians are arguing. 'Don't play with him,' the guy in the hat says, 'you ain't that good a shot." So the perfessor puts the rifle up to his jaw, takes aim for the longest time, then lowers it, then raises it again, then lowers it, and says 'I can't do it. I don't know why.' I swear to God. And get this—he was crying. A policeman crying." He took a long swig directly from the bottle. "By this time the Indian in the hat is furious and grabs the rifle, gets off a wild shot, but the prisoner—his name was Vann, I remember that—was already long gone. Can you imagine?"

"Did they go after the prisoner?"

"No, by this time Funny Hat was so disgusted, he just started trotting off in the opposite direction. And what was the other guy gonna do—run after him waving his arms and shouting 'stop thief?'" He looked steely-eyed at the reporter. "It was funny, but it wasn't funny. That Indian had no business being a policeman. And here's why: a couple of weeks later, he finally gets the gumption to shoot a bad guy, but he's such a bad shot, he kills his partner, too. Last time anybody saw him he was riding out of the Territory." He took a long theatrical sip. "Probably on his way to Californy. Hear they don't mind crying policemen out there."

A month later the *Police Gazette* ran a sarcastic article entitled "Bumbleweeds and Crying Policemen" with the subheadline "The Lesser Adventures of Lawmen on the Frontier." Edward Perryman was not mentioned by name, but every man in every barbershop in the Creek nation knew exactly who it was talking about.

BOOK TWO

BOOK TWO

CHAPTER THIRTEEN

February 11, 1898 felt like the coldest day of Tom Sixkiller's life. Rain the day before had turned into a sudden and savage ice storm overnight, converting the woods around Okmulgee into a spectacular, beautiful, and very dangerous forest of ice.

Night winds sent the frozen and brittle branches of old trees crashing to the ground, pelting everything beneath with icy shards. Falling limbs reverberated like cannon, making Sixkiller's horse skittish and hard to handle. He guided his mount away from the river where the biggest trees grew.

The chill that permeated his bones was nothing compared to the frost gathered on his dignity. Tom Sixkiller was about to find himself unemployed. He was just two months shy of his sixty-seventh birthday and had been a lawman for fifty years. Now Clem at the Indian Office told him he might want to look into farming.

Tom wasn't getting fired. In two weeks, the entire judicial system of the Five Civilized Tribes, which included all of its courts and police, was being terminated by act of Congress. The Creek lighthorse was being disbanded, along with the lighthorse from the other civilized tribes, to be replaced with an Indian

Territory lighthorse who were hired, not elected, and whose jurisdiction crossed traditional boundaries. Many Indians saw this as just the first move by the federal government to do away with the tribal system entirely; as Benjamin Perryman had written, "Killing the cat an inch at a time, starting at the tail."

The demise of the tribal lighthorsemen stemmed from both a justifiable white frustration over jurisdictional squabbles that had been going on forever, long before the tribes arrived in Indian Territory, and a colossal misreading of the Indian mind.

To whites, an Indian was an Indian. But in fact, the various members of the Five Civilized Tribes barely tolerated each other. The Choctaws and Chickasaws got along very well, sharing a root language and almost identical laws. The Creeks got along with the Seminoles, as well as any group could get along with that small and belligerent nation. But the Choctaws looked down on the Creeks as dysfunctional country cousins, and the Creeks felt the sting. And everybody disliked the Cherokees, it seemed. The Cherokees, being by far the largest of the five tribes, didn't give a damn and said so. So when the federal government established a unified Indian Territory judicial system, it solved one problem while creating others.

And one thing was certain: despite his years of experience and success, the new system had no place for Tom Sixkiller.

He dismounted in front of the Creek Council House. The two-story unpainted wood structure held the soon-to-be-abolished Creek Supreme Court, offices for the House of Kings and House of Warriors, and executive offices for the first and second chiefs.

Crunching his way across crystalline blades of grass, Tom noticed, not for the first time, that sound itself must dislike the cold as much as he did. It had disappeared, gone to ground, sought shelter, and took most of the wind with it.

The air seemed dead, the silence so complete he could hear the faint hum that he was manufacturing from within. The lonely scream of a blue jay was amplified tenfold and startled Tom to the point that he automatically dropped his hand to his revolver.

Tom was a little on edge; not because he was losing his job—that was a given—but because he had been called to meet with Chief Isparhecher. He didn't like Isparhecher, thought him ignorant, opportunistic and very probably corrupt. But he was the principal chief, and Tom had spent far too many years as a policeman to start questioning authority now.

He entered the old chief's office, which was even more sparse than Tom's, if that was possible. Isparhecher could neither read nor write, so there were no books anywhere, not even a Bible. Unlike many other full-bloods, the chief had not converted to Christianity.

The chief sat in one of four rustic chairs pulled up around a Franklin stove. He motioned Tom over Indian-style, with the downward sweep of his hand usually reserved for children. Tom noticed, but didn't take offense.

Isparhecher was dressed in the old style of the full-bloods: long white cotton shirt that draped almost to his knees, a colorful cloth sash tied at his waist, doeskin leggings, and a white turban pinned with a medallion made of straw. He wore this kind of clothing for effect back home, but on his frequent visits to Washington he was proud to wear the suit and starched collar of the white man. When a White House aide once asked him to wear a blanket to a congressional hearing, he was so offended that he stomped out, returned to his hotel and stayed drunk for three days.

"Come sit down, Captain. It is good to see you. We have much in common these days, you and I." Tom nodded and waited. Isparhecher coughed up a mirthless laugh. "Here we are, the captain of a disappeared lighthorse and me, chief of a disappearing nation."

Tom sat stiffly on the edge of a chair. "You are much respected by your people, and we are many," he said politely.

"Yes, we are many. But now we run around like chickens, and the accursed white man throws allotments at us and says, 'Here, don't listen to the rooster. Eat all you want.'"

"The people elected you our chief. We will listen."

"No, they only listen to the white man's song, which is money. I am now a rooster with a thousand hens and no beak. I have no money, I can't pay you, I can't pay anybody. But I have some plans." He hesitated, realizing he had been talking only about himself. "What about you and your men? What are you going to do?"

Tom slid back in his chair. "Well, I got Chitto a job on the Katy as a bull. He didn't want to do it at first, but the idea of beating up white men appealed to him. Dan Fixico got his allotment, ran down to Muskogee and sold it to the land grabbers, then took his money and his ugly hat to Texas. San Antonio, I heard."

The chief leaned forward. "What about you?"

"I took my allotment, but I don't even know where it is. Over near Wetumka somewhere. The railroads don't want it. It may be good for farming, I don't know, but I do know a farm takes a farmer, and I'm flat out of those. I'd probably be the first farmer to starve to death standing behind a plow."

Isparhecher rose, perhaps to demonstrate his superiority. "Look, I take care of my friends. And you, too, Captain." His laugh this time was robust and real. "I know, I am sure you don't like me. Many do not. But I trust you, you will do as I ask. I have important work for you. I want you to head the new

Creek Census Commission. And it is a job unlike many these days: you will keep me informed but answer to and be paid by the Indian Office. The best of all worlds for you, I think."

Tom was slow to answer. "I am a lawman, *Micco*. I know how to do that. But doing a census of our people? I am poor at reading and writing. How can I take a census?"

"There is money to hire a few people who will do the writing for you. Any of your out-of-work lighthorsemen know how to write English?"

"I can think of one," Tom said. "But I still would have no idea what to do."

"That is all right. Take your time. You can learn as you go." The chief lowered his voice conspiratorially. "And the longer it takes you, the better it is for our people."

"I don't understand."

"You and I are facing a snake, ready to strike. I recently returned from Washington. Congress, especially Senator Curtis, wants the allotments to be finished. And of course, when the allotments are done, so is the Creek nation. The white man won't need us anymore. But the Dawes Commission cannot finish the allotments until it finishes the census of the tribes. The Choctaws are dragging their feet, and I intend to do the same. We are making great progress in Washington to restore our treaties of 1872, but we need time. You will give me that time. So be thorough. Send reports to the Dawes Commission, but make sure they are incomplete. Keep the snake at bay. Call them ... preliminary. Say some pages got lost. We can stall this census for years and regain the strength of our nation." He pointed his finger rudely at Tom. "And I will regain my beak."

◆ ◆ ◆

Like so many other times in the old chief's reign, he misread Congressional resolve. This time it would have ruinous consequences.

CHAPTER FOURTEEN

Edward Perryman had finally found his niche.

Despite his continuing helpless dreams that inevitably ended with Jubal dying in his arms, he began to assuage his anger and feelings of loss by throwing himself into a new reality. The law suited him. He could never bring Jubal back, but he could honor him as his friend had requested.

Clerking for ArkansasJjudge John Whitten during the day, reading law books at night, Edward found studying for the law enjoyable, interesting, and frankly, quite easy. He knew he had an excellent memory, but had never known exactly how to apply it until now. At last the bitter taste of failure was leaving his mouth.

He was acknowledged to be the best law clerk in Little Rock; all the judges in the capital courthouse agreed. After only a year of reading the law, and with the encouragement of his mentor Judge Whitten, Edward took the Arkansas state bar examination. The test results would not be released until mid-June, but on this barefoot day in May, Edward sat on the courthouse lawn eating fried chicken, confident that he had not just passed, but aced the bar exams. He wrapped himself in courtroom dreams.

Even if he had been listening rather than wool-gathering, Edward would never have heard the man who came up behind him. "Edward Perryman! Hello, young fellow. I've been looking for you."

Edward swung around, wielding a drumstick like a crude weapon. "Captain Sixkiller? You nearly scared me to death. What a surprise!" He laid the chicken down on the newspaper he had been reading and stood. Wiping his hands on his handkerchief, he dropped his voice. "I wasn't sure you would ever want to see me again, Captain."

"It's just plain Tom Sixkiller now, Edward. My lighthorsing days are behind me."

"Apologies, sir, but I could no more call you Tom than I could call my father Ben. You earned your rank with me, sir." Edward wondered if he had brought up a sore subject and added, "I'm sorry, I hope my mention of rank doesn't offend you. I read about all the tribal lighthorse being forced to disband and then being rolled into one for the whole territory. Think that will help? Maybe ease some jurisdictional disputes?"

"An Indian still can't arrest a white man. That's the weasel in the chicken coop."

"Speaking of which, care for a piece of fried chicken?" Edward offered.

Sixkiller examined the pile of remains on the newspaper and chuckled. "Just like when I was a kid—backs, wings and necks. Well, being the youngest of four boys, I grew partial to necks." He picked one up and stripped a bit of meat off the underside. "I might have to grow fond of them again unless I can get your help, young Perryman. Care to take a walk?"

"You can walk with me to the judge's chambers. We have a two o'clock hearing, but until then I'm all yours, sir. How can I help you?"

They crossed a leafy square that seemed to have been taken over by scolding squirrels. Tom Sixkiller looked up into the trees with that hundred-mile stare that Edward knew meant listen and keep quiet. "I have a new job, a job your father tells me I am colossally unqualified for—he sends his regards, by the way—but it's an important job, and I must admit I've grown partial to eating regular."

The old man put his hand on Edward's shoulder exactly as Benjamin Perryman did in moments of intimacy. Edward was even more astonished by this gesture than he had been by Sixkiller's surprise appearance. "I've been asked by that old reprobate chief Isparhecher to conduct the official census of our people for the Dawes Commission." He waved his hand dismissively in front of his face. "Now, I understand that working for the Dawes Commission can leave a taste in your mouth like sucking on an old penny, but sometimes you can't choose your partner."

Edward said, "I've been reading a lot about the federal government putting pressure on the Dawes Commission to get a census of each of the tribes. I also hear that the census-taking is not going well."

Sixkiller looked approvingly at the young man. "You have a civil tongue, Edward, I like that. Yep, every tribe is way behind schedule. The Choctaws say they were unable to provide a complete roll because they lost much of their work in a fire; the Chickasaws are looking for a match and kindling; the Cherokees say they need to debate it a little bit more—three years just haven't been enough; and the Seminoles handed over a census that included dead men, dogs and a few chickens. The court took one look and threw it back."

"What about us Creeks?"

Sixkiller scoffed. "Like everything else in our unhappy

nation, it is an ax being swung by a child. It might hit its target, or it might cut off its own foot. Isparhecher and most of the full-bloods believe the census is a bad idea, and the way to defeat it is to delay, debate, take votes, and send delegations here and there until the Dawes Commission finally throws up its hands in disgust and goes away. Isparhecher knows I can't read or write much better than he can. That may be why he hired me—he figured it would take me forever. At least that's Benjamin's fix on it."

Edward stopped, narrowed his eyes with suspicion, and turned to face Sixkiller. "So ... naturally you come looking for a man who failed at being a lighthorseman to help you fail as a census taker?"

"Now, none of that, son," the old Indian said. "Just the opposite. You are smart—smarter than the rest of us lighthorsemen put together, I am thinking. I didn't come all the way to Arkansas so you could help me fail. I need you to help us succeed. We stand to be crushed. Isparhecher doesn't want to know how the white man thinks, because he feels the white man is crazy and values nothing. But I have spent years with the white man and know that he possesses, in abundance, something the old full-bloods cannot understand: impatience. The people behind the Dawes Commission want the censuses to be completed, and nothing can stop it now. If you and I don't give the Dawes Commission a census, the commissioners will lose patience and do it themselves, and they will make a mess of it. Many of our people will be left with nothing. No land, no money, no home; hell, no tribe. That's where it's leading, you know.

"We will be paid directly by the commission, so that is good. Isparhecher says the nation is broke, as he takes yet another trip to Washington to plead with Congress and eat high at the fancy hotels, but I have enough money for you and a few more. Benjamin has found me a young woman from a college to handle the books, and I hired Monday Grayson to take the census in the freedman towns like Northfork, Calumet and Canadian. Most of the mixed-bloods are already on the rolls, but we will have to work hard to get to the full-bloods. That's where I come in, because I'm full-blood too and most of the people know me. They will talk to me and you can get the information you need to finish the census. We must succeed, and I can do it with someone I know and trust. Can I count on you?"

Edward kicked an imaginary pebble, then looked up. "Yes, Captain, of course you can. Nothing would please me more. Please give me a couple of weeks to clean up a few things with the judge and I'll meet you back in Okmulgee."

Edward simply could not wait to see his father again. He checked in at the newspaper, but Miss Thompson, who wrote up the want ads, told him Benjamin had already headed for home.

Edward found his father sitting on the front porch swing much as he left him a year earlier. To Edward's eye, Benjamin Perryman never got older, just more compact. His mother, Elizabeth, used to joke that Benjamin would never die, he'd just skinny himself into the next world.

Edward ran up the porch steps and uncharacteristically embraced his father.

Smiling broadly, Benjamin fiddled with his glasses to regain composure. "Welcome back, son. Hail the conquering hero. I have certainly missed you." He patted his breast pocket.

"Got a letter for you, Edward old man," he said in his home-cooking baritone. "It's from ... let's see...," he pulled the envelope out of his coat pocket and looked at it theatrically. "Oh, that's right, the Arkansas Bar Association. Want to have a look?"

Edward loved this horseplay. "No thanks, Father. Mind if I take a load off and sit with you? Why would I want to read the most important letter in my life when I could sit here with you and count fireflies?"

"Good question; but truth be known, I'm a mite curious. Of course, I've been looking at this danged envelope for three days. I think it's high time."

Edward opened the envelope by carefully slicing the edge with a pocket knife. He studied the letter intently, then slowly lowered it to his lap. His face was stone. He waited a few heartbeats. "I passed. I am a lawyer. At least in Arkansas."

"Well, by God!" Benjamin shouted. "By God, you did it. That means you are a lawyer here too, of course." He patted Edward on the shoulder. "And it's lucky for me. Otherwise I have no idea what I would have done with the enormous rhubarb pie I've got cooling in the kitchen."

Edward's eyes widened in delight. His father had remembered it was Edward's favorite. "Thank you, Father."

"You are welcome. I thought this might be the way your mother would have celebrated if she were still here."

"We could set a place for her, pretend like the whole family is celebrating."

Benjamin hesitated, then looked lovingly into his son's eyes. "This may sound crazy to you, Edward, but the Indian part of me doesn't care for that idea. The dead need to remain apart. I think of your mother every day, but I think of her now in the spirit world. That's where she belongs." He paused. "But that does remind me. The woman I recruited to help you and Tom keep the census numbers is here in town, got in Thursday. Her name is Maud Fisher, and she's real nice. She's living with Mrs. Stallcup—it was Mrs. Stallcup who made the pie, actually." He looked down at his feet and then stammered just a bit. "I might have mentioned you coming home and .. maybe, you know ... said something about her coming over for dinner to meet you and help celebrate your passing the bar." He saw Edward suspiciously look down at the letter and laughed. "Come now, as if there was ever any doubt? I could have guessed long before you opened that letter; and then when Judge Whitten wrote that you scored in the top ten percent, that sort of let the cat out of the bag. I am proud. So what do you say? Want to meet your new partner?"

"Sounds like a command performance, but that would be fine," said Edward. "We'd meet tomorrow in any case. What is she like? Fat, skinny, young, old, sings opera, plays the banjo, reads French, smokes ready-mades? Anything?"

"You lawyers are all the same, asking too many questions. Let me just say you won't be disappointed. Now you go out back and wash up while I fetch the young lady."

When Benjamin brought the young woman into the kitchen, parts of Edward's brain went into a love cramp that reduced his thought processes to the Indian corn soup called *sofki*.

"Hello," she said. "I'm Maud Fisher. You must be Edward, my colleague and newly-minted attorney. Congratulations."

Edward stared for a second, then shook her hand like he was pumping water. "Yes, we're having rhubarb pie. For my mother. Instead of my mother." He wanted to cut out his tongue.

"Sounds like a real celebration," she answered softly. "May I sit?"

Maud Fisher was the whitest white woman Edward had ever seen. She wouldn't be called pretty. Like Tolstoy's happy families, all pretty women were pretty the same. But Maud's face danced close to beauty, was beautiful in a certain light, and was hers alone. Her light-brown hair was fine, a bit unruly with wisps escaping down her alabaster temples and long neck. She had a slightly lop-sided, thin-lipped smile that might have made her seem girlish until you saw the eyes. They were wide-set, cornflower blue—a rarity in Indian Territory—with flecks of gold that captured the light and threw it back at you with wit and curiosity.

Benjamin could see that if conversation was going to occur, he would need to lead it until Edward could corral his thoughts. He turned his newspaper skills toward interviewing the two young people, making them feel comfortable without even noticing that they hardly spoke directly to each other. They talked of Shakespeare, the land rushes in neighboring Oklahoma Territory, railroads, how to milk a cow (Maud had spent a summer on a Wisconsin farm), and the emerging territorial laws and regulations. They talked through stew, they talked through the notorious rhubarb pie, they talked through coffee, and still they talked. Finally, Benjamin stood. "We've all got a big day in front of us. Let's adjourn for now," he said. "Edward, why don't you walk the young lady home? I'll clean up here."

The moon was so bright they could see their shadows on the wide dirt street. Edward redeemed himself somewhat by becoming a tour guide, pointing out trees, flowers and buildings she had most likely already seen.

When they reached Mrs. Stallcup's front porch, Edward took a deep breath. Here is what he wanted to say: "I had a splendid evening. There is a small request I'd like to make before you go inside. Will you marry me, bear my children, live with me in joy, then stroke my brow as I die of old age in your arms?"

Here's what he did say: "I had a splendid evening, Miss Fisher. I will come for you early tomorrow. I will introduce you to Captain Sixkiller."

Maud put her hand lightly on Edward's arm. "I'll be ready, Edward," she said quietly. Not for the last time. Edward felt she was reading his mind, answering his first request.

CHAPTER FIFTEEN

Testimony (through interpreter) *before the United States Senate Committee on Indian Affairs, Honorable Richard Pettigrew presiding.*
Thursday, July 14, 1898

Senator Pettigrew: The chair recognizes Eufala Harjo, member of the Muskogee Creek Indian tribe. Mister Harjo.

Eufala Harjo: Sir, my people, we are pushed out of all that we had. The full-blood Indian people are pushed out today and they have left their homes, and taken what they have and everything and are camped out in the woods today. Their homes and land are all taken and now the Indians are all outside nearly. It is going to be cold weather after awhile, and there is the women and the little children and the old people, and we don't know what to do with them or where to get a house to put them in. All the property such as cattle and hogs and horses—it is all gone and we have not got anything left. We used to have plenty and more than we wanted and now we have not got anything.

Pettigrew: Is that not because you have declined to take your allotment or occupy the land you were allotted, and having declined to take the land offered to you free and clear, that land has been allotted to someone else?

Harjo: They have taken my farm away from me and the house that I built. Another woman got my farm and she sold it to a white man and they have that farm and they are working it last year. I am very sad and I hope the white fathers will help the Indians.

Pettigrew: Why didn't you take your allotment?

Harjo: I didn't take it because I wanted my treaty rights, for I loved them. I loved the old treaty. The old treaty said my people would own the land together, like a mighty tree, not given to each leaf. The leaves will be blown away.

Pettigrew: I am afraid the die is cast, sir. When you refused to accept this government's generous offer, you sealed your fate. We will do what we can, of course.

Chitto was having the dream again. He had dreamed it so many times he knew it forwards and backwards. He dreamed it half-awake when he sat in the afternoon sun under the old tree near his cabin. He dreamed it some mornings, especially when he was hungry. He could call up his dream whenever he wanted to, but he never wanted to. It frightened him.

Chitto had lost his job with the railroad after only three months. He had gotten into a fight with a white railroad guard who had kicked Chitto for letting another Indian slip off a freight car. The white guard was a head taller and carried a baton, but Chitto had knocked him senseless, dragged him under one of the wagons at the far end of the Ft. Gibson rail station platform, and disappeared wordlessly back into the hills above Okmulgee where he had been born.

In Chitto's dream, he is in a rowboat in a reed-banked lake with water the color of tea. His father is in another boat close by, but Chitto cannot reach him. He has to shout across at the older man.

"Father, you may not fish here any longer. We must leave this part of the lake."

His father laughs at the absurdity of the request. "My son, you know this is our spot. It was my father's spot, and his father's spot. Someday it will be your spot. Come into my boat. The fishing is good; they cannot see us in this water."

Chitto begins to cry. "I cannot come. This fishing hole no longer is ours, it was given to a white man. We may never fish here again. You must leave forever."

The old man stands in the bow of his boat. "This is my spot. This is our spot. It has always been so." He gives a dream-smile and a cheerful wave. "If I can no longer catch the fish, I will join them." He dives into the murky water, leaving only a brief bubbly trail.

Chitto wants to dive into the lake to save his father, but he cannot get out of his little boat. He struggles and finally awakens, bathed in sweat and self-loathing.

He didn't need a *hilis haya* to interpret this. It was a death dream, not for his already-dead father, but for the part of him that might or might not enter the spirit world. Chitto didn't know what to do, but like most Indians he felt that by joining others, their collective will would give them power.

And he found a group to join. In a classic example of unintended consequences, the Dawes Commission did something that the Indians had for thousands of years failed to do themselves—brought the full-bloods of the Civilized Tribes together in common cause.

It was called the Four Mothers Society. No one seemed to know exactly where it started, probably among the Choctaws, but word swept through the full-bloods like a prairie fire. They would announce their meetings as they did in the old days: a runner would arrive at one of the small, still mostly Indian towns far from the railroads and cattle pens. He would give the town chief a small bundle of sticks that would indicate the number of days until a meeting, and the name of a gathering place like Atoka or Tuskahoma.

Chitto left his little cabin to attend a Four Mothers Society meeting at the stomp ground near the tiny Thlacco town on the South Canadian River. To his astonishment, there were hundreds of men and women milling about; some collecting money, some speaking, some just nodding in agreement. There was a fatalistic realism among the speakers. They realized they were now outriders in a white man's world, but their purpose was to confuse, disrupt and delay the count for another week, another month, another year.

This felt good to Chitto and he started traveling the backwoods to attend other meetings. He became a familiar face among the Four Mothers leaders. Finally, one day in the old grape arbors outside of Wetumka, he was approached by a man named Bonaparte, who seemed to be the Society's leader. "I know you," Bonaparte said. "You are the lighthorseman who rode with Captain Sixkiller. You are Chitto, the snake. Welcome. I have need of you, if you are interested."

The two men walked a short distance away from the stomp ground and found a convenient rock. "Chitto, the Four Mothers Society is a peaceful group," Bonaparte said. "But we must acknowledge the realities of who and what we are. We are many now, perhaps more than five thousand." Chitto whistled in appreciation. "Our members give money to sustain us, send us to Washington, pay for our challenges in the federal courts and, I am sorry to say, fight corruption among some of the very people we elected to serve us. It is never enough money, but it is a lot of money. It is not unusual for me to have two or three thousand dollars in my office. That is an enticing sum. And as we become more successful, we are attracting men who want to see us fail. Men who are willing to help us fail. At gun point."

"Have you been threatened?" asked Chitto.

"Yes, and robbed once," Bonaparte said. "I am well aware of the exploits of the Creek lighthorsemen, and I regret their passing. But the white deputies will not lift a finger to help us. The Four Mothers Society is growing as large as some tribes. It is time we had our own police. Chitto, would you consider becoming the captain of the Four Mothers Lighthorse?"

"You honor me," said Chitto, and felt his spirit rising out of the small boat at last.

CHAPTER SIXTEEN

"I am somewhat confused," Maud said. She speared a tiny slice of watermelon with her fork. "It's been less than a month into our work, yet Tam Bixby at the Commission thinks we are dawdling, Chief Isparhecher says we are going too fast, and now there is this new group—the Four ... Sisters?—set on keeping all the tribes from signing off on the census? If the rock doesn't get us, perhaps the hard place will." She shook her head slowly. "Don't we have *anyone* to champion our cause?"

"Four Mothers," Edward said absently. He was listening yet not listening, perhaps more intent than necessary on his colleague's eating habits. He had never seen a person eat watermelon with a fork before. It seemed incredibly dainty. When he and his young friends ate watermelon at school or church socials, they would reluctantly use spoons, making watermelon caves in their slices and using the spoons as catapults to launch sticky missiles against schoolmates and other enemies. More often, however, Edward and his buddies would tackle a cool slice barehanded. They would make their way through the layers—first through the exquisitely sweet heart, then through the ammunition-laden seed layer, then gnaw their way down like beavers through the pink into the white. That night, Edward was back to the spoon.

Benjamin hosted Edward, Maud, Tom Sixkiller and Enid Thompson from the newspaper. They sat around the long trestle table in Benjamin's backyard, finishing a watermelon that only recently had been cooling in the stream out back. The long-suffering Miss Thompson (who had never been called Enid to anyone's recollection) was there as Maud's chaperone, but she was also puttering between kitchen and backyard, play-acting the hostess. Miss Thompson had been quietly in love with Benjamin for years, but she had long ago traded intimacy for proximity. In her heart of hearts, she accepted the trade. Men often frightened her.

Like at that moment, for instance. Tom Sixkiller was nonchalantly eating his watermelon with his Bowie knife. Benjamin noted the fear and fascination in the eyes of both Miss Thompson and Maud, and handed Tom a large spoon. "Here, Tom," he chuckled. "You're going to have a smile cut from ear to ear if you don't watch out."

Tom sheathed his dagger and laughed. "Guess you are right, Ben. My smile is already so ugly it scares little children. Wouldn't want to make it any bigger." He nodded to Miss Thompson. "Thanks for the chicken and dumplings, ma'am. Edward and I are headed out to where supper is likely to be a choice between two dishes: beans and biscuits, or biscuits and beans."

"The Four Mothers," Benjamin muttered to himself. "What a sweet name for a train wreck."

Tom, who was never able to sit still for long, stood quietly and stretched his old bones. He started pacing, then seemed to begin talking to the trees. "You know, there is something about me that wants to admire those fools. But fools they are, wrapped in the frayed blankets of their ancestors. This isn't our world any more. That's hard to swallow, but we are too few. Those full-blood fools are talking to each other about staying out of the rain while a tornado as wide as a barn and black as a bruise is headed right for them."

"But the captain and I have a plan to use the members of the Four Mothers to advance our efforts," Edward said, enthusiastic at last. "We intend to go to the Four Mothers powwows, set up our tents and field tables, and enroll the adults then and there."

"It was mostly your idea, Edward. And a fine one," said Tom. "Rumors tend to wither and die in the glare of the sun. Edward and I will represent the truth and we will sign the members up. Maybe not all at once, but eventually. They may be fools, but they're not stupid. And they're my fools."

"You mentioned rumors?" Maud asked, looking first at Tom Sixkiller and then at Edward. She rested her hand lightly on Edward's shoulder, a tiny gesture that everyone noticed and no one mentioned.

Edward answered, "The rumor sweeping the back woods is that if you sign the rolls, you are agreeing to give up your home and be assigned an allotment far away. That is not the purpose of the census."

"Not yet," Benjamin said softly.

Edward spread his fingers wide. "What can we do, Father? Congress has instructed the Dawes Commission to enroll every Indian in every tribe. This will be done. And either we do it or the Dawes Commission will hire white men to do it for us, turning a problem into a disaster. We must do it, and do it as well as we can." He leaned back and absently tapped the table with the fingers of one hand. "And what if the census does become the basis for allotments? If you are not on the rolls, you will no longer exist in a court of law. You will have no rights, no old treaties to protect you. You will have no land, and when you turn to your tribe for help…."

Tom's voice was rough and unpleasant. "You will find that your nation has no land either, no courts, no police, no schools, no money. Only ghosts of the past. We must conduct the census to protect us from ourselves."

Maud smiled. "I had a professor at Wheaton who said that the enemy of a good plan is the perfect plan; and there is no such thing as a perfect plan. You have a good plan, gentlemen. Execute it and we will be ready to assist you."

Isparhecher had offered the old lighthorse police barracks for the census team, but Benjamin convinced Tom that the already-leery Indians might feel doubly so at going there to sign up. Instead, Benjamin donated space in the front of the newspaper office. Maud liked very much setting up shop in the newspaper. She had a desk, bookcases filling fast with papers, and ledger books so big it took effort to open them. She would take notebooks, tablets and scraps of paper with census data delivered to her by Tom, Edward, and Monday Grayson, and carefully enter the information into the official ledgers.

Maud had quite a few things to transcribe: the date; the name, age, sex and blood quantum of the individual; tribe or freedman designation; place of residence; and names of mother and father. She would transfer the information onto the ledger in her well-tutored handwriting in black ink. When each page was completed, Tom would place a stamp provided to him by the Dawes Commission on it and, with no little pride, sign his name—a skill only recently acquired.

Maud found the work tedious, but necessarily so, and honestly could think of no one in Okmulgee more suited to the task. She had come to help the Indians, and thanks to Benjamin Perryman, was doing so at last.

She had grown very fond of Edward. He was witty, smart, and a little bashful. She also adored, even envied, Edward's solid relationship with his father. She might have been daydreaming about Edward as the father of her children when he startled her by bursting into the newspaper with a lunch of fried catfish, cole slaw and peaches.

"Home is the hungry sailor; home from the South Canadian," Edward boomed, holding the wicker basket aloft.

Maud laughed. "And home is the hunter from the census. You brought us lunch, you sweet man?"

"No more for me, Edward," Miss Thompson said mischievously. Her desk was set behind the big glass case filled with pens, inks and paper. "I swear I couldn't eat another bite. You two youngsters scoot. I'll mind the ledger."

Edward and Maud walked down to the sun-dappled Big Little Creek, a name that made perfect sense to an Indian. One would not want to confuse it with Little Little Creek, a mile to the south.

They found an outcropping of granite that slid into the water, creating a tiny pool where leaves from the nearby sycamores eddied. In a gesture of Indian Territory chivalry, Edward had packed napkins and a blanket. Also forks.

After lunch they laid on the blanket, looking into the slowly swaying trees and listening to birdsong and katydids. Edward reached over and casually, far too casually, patted Maud on the hand, then let his hand rest there.

"Do you mind?" he asked, blood throbbing in his ears.

Maud sat upright and turned to face him. "Does this answer

your question?" She kissed him softly, lingeringly, on the lips. It was a closed-mouth kiss, conveying prologue and promise rather than passion, but it stunned Edward nevertheless. He had never been kissed before. Come to think of it, he couldn't even remember seeing people kiss in real life, although he was acutely aware of the premise.

Edward wanted to respond, but was in an emotional wilderness. Instinctively he conjured up the only tender exchange between a man and a woman he had ever seen, Billy Mingo running his rough hand over the face of his wife, memorizing her features just before his death. Edward ran his fingers lightly over Maud's face, which she had lifted slightly in anticipation. "I want to know everything about you, Maud Fisher ... your face, your thoughts, your secrets, your ... well, your everything." Shyness overcame him and he sprang to his feet, throwing his arms wide to indicate the scope of his inquiry, and almost stepped into the creek, causing Maud to giggle.

He caught himself in time and dropped athletically to his knees beside her again, relieved that the spell was broken and yet desperately hoping it would return. "Let's start with college," he said. "Tell me about Wheaton College. Is it an agricultural school? Do both men and women attend, or women only? What did you study?"

Maud, playful now, pulled him back down beside her. The picnic basket served as a bundling board between them. "Why do you think it's an agricultural school? Oh, you mean because of the Wheaton part? No, that's just the name of a rich evangelical bishop who donated the land and built the first building. When Wheaton was started a hundred years ago, just about the entire faculty was composed of evangelical preachers. The townspeople used to call the school 'missionary meadows.' But it was nondenominational and very progressive. It was one of the first colleges in the country to graduate women, and Negroes were enrolled at Wheaton ten years before the Emancipation Proclamation. During the Civil War, Wheaton became one of the most important stops on the underground railroad. I received an excellent education."

"Did you study to be a preacher, too?"

Maud picked a dandelion and examined it. "No, I just didn't feel the calling. But that was my father's great wish for me. He is a protestant minister in Dayton, Ohio. Semi-retired now. He wanted me to be a missionary in China or Africa or some other dark place. He and my mother spent three years as missionaries in the Belgian Congo before I was born, and he often talked of that time as the highlight of his life." Her brow furrowed. "I think he is disappointed in me. He never looks at me the way your father looks at you."

"What does your mother think?"

"That's where you and I have something in common," Maud said, tossing the flower into the water. "My mother passed away when I was young, too. She died from the effects of some tropical disease she brought home from Africa. I was only five, so I don't remember her at all. It's funny; I remember the funeral, every terrifying second of it, but not my mother. I sometimes try to picture her face, but it is no use." She clapped her hands together, once, as if rousing herself from her reverie. "Maybe I'm lucky. You can't grieve for someone who never existed."

"Grief skipped me, too," said Edward. "I think my father consumed the Perryman family allotment. Partly to protect me. But he couldn't consume my anger. It got me in trouble, of course, but that's a story for another day."

"Would that story have to do with Jubal Bull?"

Edward didn't flinch. His only physical reaction was a

slight flush in his face. "I figured someone would tell you about that sooner or later. Yes, Jubal was my best friend, best friend in school, best friend in the lighthorse. We rode together, we ate together, we dreamed together, and I killed him. An accident, but he died. It crushed me, Maud. I left the lighthorsemen, I left Indian Territory, I wanted to leave everything. But I couldn't leave Jubal. He was proud of me. As he lay dying, he made me promise to study the law. A dying wish must be honored. And, of course, it changed my life. Jubal never stopped being my friend, and neither did Captain Sixkiller."

"You are surrounded by friends, Edward."

He smiled. "Fate has a way, I guess. If I ever have a son, I'm going to name him Jubal."

"It's a beautiful name, Edward," Maud said. "It means rejoice."

Edward was filled with fond remembrance. "I'm surprised it doesn't mean talkative. Jubal had the gift of tongue. I wish he could have met you."

She put a searching hand on Edward's cheek. "I've been wanting to do that ever since you touched *my* face."

Edward lightly took her hand in both of his own. "How did fate bring you here? There must have been a hundred places for a beautiful college graduate to go. Why here?"

"Indian Territory. In the abstract, I suppose I chose it to please my father, or at least not to displease him further. It wasn't Africa, but from Dayton, Ohio it sounded exotic. But when I told my father my decision, he laughed dryly and said that theologically, at least, that field had been plowed. The place was crawling with Baptists. And white people. The only thing Indian about Indian Territory these days is its name, he said. But with the help of my advisors at Wheaton—those rascal farmers—I got a placement teaching English and music at Kendall College in Muskogee."

"You taught music? You are a musician?"

"Yes, I play the piano, which is an unnecessary skill in Okmulgee at the moment. Frankly, it wasn't much use at Kendall either. My English classes were well-attended, but only four young women showed up for my music lessons, and every one of them was white. I hated to admit it, but my father was more right than wrong, at least in Muskogee. So when your father showed up asking for help working alongside real Indians, on a project to help all Indians, I jumped at the chance. And *ta-da*, here I am."

"And I can't tell you how happy I am that you are." His face lit up. "And I can start working on a piano! They have one over in Wewoka, though unfortunately it's at the whorehouse … I, um, I guess. So I hear."

They collapsed in laughter that soon turned to an embrace and a fiery, probing kiss.

CHAPTER SEVENTEEN

The treaty of 1866 between the United States and the Creeks was a treaty between victor and vanquished, and was every bit as harsh as one might imagine. For instance, the Creeks were forced to sell an area half the size of Connecticut to the Seminoles, for pennies an acre. The Seminoles had themselves lost huge chunks of land to the Sac and Fox.

The 1866 treaty also stated that all blacks residing in the Creek nation, called freedmen—most of whom were emancipated or runaway slaves—were entitled to full tribal membership, with all voting privileges. But although Creek freedmen may have been members of the tribe pursuant to government order, many full-bloods refused to accept this status. So the freedmen, like outliers throughout history, formed diasporas in Muskogee, Tulsa, and other railhead towns, and created from whole cloth the so-called "black towns" of Deep Fork, North Fork and, later, Beggs, Bolie, and Calumet. This added isolation to suspicion.

So for thirty years the relationship between the freedmen and the full-blood Creeks had teetered between uneasy and tense.

And then came the census.

◆ ◆ ◆

Tom Sixkiller returned from a moderately successful signing after two days at a Four Mothers Society powwow at the old Alabama Town stomp ground. His casual, undemanding style had garnered him 70 names—70 hard-shell, non-English-speaking skeptics—so he felt like his and Edward's plan was working.

He walked into the newspaper office waving his list like a peace treaty. "Not bad, Tom, old man," Benjamin said, going over the ledger with Maud, "but that's just about what Monday Grayson gets on an average day. That man is a veritable census factory."

"His lot is an easier one," Tom tried to point out. "Freedmen are eager to sign. They can double their wives' allotment with the stroke of a pen."

"Yes, I understand that; but still. You've been looking at every page of that ledger for correctness and proof of citizenship, but Maud and I started keeping tally on the total sign-ups. How many freedmen does Grayson have, Maud?"

"At last count, one thousand two hundred fourteen," Maud answered.

"And that's in less than four months," Benjamin said. "Grayson is over at Deep Fork this week. Maybe you should take a trip over there to see how he's doing it."

Tom was thoughtful. "I think I'll do that," he said. "And for the time being let's keep those numbers to ourselves. If Isparhecher finds out there are more than a thousand enrolled and voting freedmen in the nation, he's likely to get jumpy, fire all of us and shut the whole thing down. Dawes Commission or no Dawes Commission."

The little village of Deep Fork was scattered along the river of the same name, which this time of year was mostly trickles, muddy pools and sandbars. The picked-over cotton fields cast a wintery finality to the countryside, but the village itself was bustling with humanity.

At the center of that humanity was Monday Grayson. Sitting behind a desk, looking out at the entrance of his white canvas field tent, Grayson gave the appearance of a benevolent king receiving petitioners. Children played and raced around in front of the tent; women with baskets of flatbread, fritters and little meat pies offered their wares; and on the porch of the nearby general store, a banjo player and his dancing daughter performed for pennies tossed in a hat on the floor. Calmly lined up in front of Grayson were a dozen or so men and women, chatting and laughing.

Tom was astonished. He had just spent two days chasing pockets of full-blood families through scrub oaks and cedars to sign them, and here was something he could barely comprehend: a census fair.

He approached. "Hey, Monday. You giving away free money or something? Circus coming to town?"

Monday Grayson smiled and waved. He was stout on the cusp of being fat, with a ready smile on his broad ebony face. "Hey, Captain." (Grayson had never served in the lighthorse, but the entire census crew had taken to calling Tom "Captain." Tom either didn't notice or simply approved. He had carried the title for forty years, after all.) "Yeah, things are going real good. I'm just about through here, then Calumet and Bolie, and I should be wrapped up by the harvest moon."

Tom entered the tent and clapped his hand on Monday's shoulder. "Take a walk with me?"

"Sure, Captain." He called over a young man in the back of the tent. "Hey, Junior, come take my place for a little while, will you? Captain and I are going to walk over and get a bite to eat."

They grabbed some flatbread and walked to a bench on the side of the general store. Tom shook his head in disbelief. "No disrespect, Monday, but are you sure all these people you are enrolling are members of the tribe? Can there really be that much difference between full-bloods and freedmen? I got to chase them down; you can't seem to get away from them."

Monday grew serious. "I had thought a lot about that, especially at first, hearing all the problems you and Edward were having. I did catch a few fakers, but very few. I'm very careful. Most of the freedmen are indeed men, so I ask them in Creek about their mother's clan, their wife's clan, where they are living and for how long. It's rare that I catch a liar." He fiddled with his flatbread. "You asked why there could be such a difference between full-bloods and freedmen and the answer—for this one thing—is tradition. You have to remember that many freedmen, and most certainly their mammas or their pappies, were slaves. They understand the value of property because they were themselves property at one time, bought and sold like cattle. That's an unforgettable lesson, Captain."

"I hadn't thought of it quite that way," Tom admitted. "We think of land as belonging to the tribe. We work the land but don't own it, so it's ours only as long as we work it. White men don't understand this."

"Neither do freedmen, truth be told. We called it sharecropping. Bad history there."

Tom looked into the trees as he so often did when thinking on his feet. "Plus we got this damn rumor running around that if you are put on the Dawes rolls, you may be forced to leave where you are living, and be allotted land somewhere else."

Monday's broad face broke into a smile. "We've heard the

same rumor, Captain, and we are delighted. 160 acres free and clear? Why, hell, that's our dream. No more working for the white man. And of course we have no long family history to consider, no burial grounds, no tradition. We like being Creeks, wouldn't have it any other way, but we want to be Creek landowners. What do they say—one man's meat is another man's poison?"

Tom stood and brushed crumbs off his pants. "I think I understand a little better now. But I hope you understand Creek politics. You need to be very careful. Chief Isparhecher doesn't trust you to begin with. He thinks you vote with the mixed-bloods because you both think like white men—and he hates white men. And I know for a fact that he doesn't have any idea how many freedmen there are. If he thought there were more than a thousand of you enrolled and ready to vote, there is no telling what he is capable of. I know you have town *miccos* just like all Creek towns, but beyond that I don't know much. I think your freedmen town *miccos* should pick a leader among themselves to go tell the old chief that you support him and don't wish him harm."

"Thank you for that excellent advice, Captain, but we're way ahead of you." Monday chuckled. "We have, and I am it."

Edward rode into the town of Okfuskee in a wagon loaded with a tent, field table, chair, pencils and paper, and sandwiches. He was prepared to be patient. He had done this many times before, relying on natural Indian curiosity to gather onlookers and, he hoped, signatures. As he approached the stomp grounds, he knew that this day might be even slower than usual, because Okfuskee was in the heart of what might be thought of as Four Mothers Society territory, a full-blood island in the ever-rising ocean of white.

He was a bit surprised to see a large gray field tent on the edge of the stomp ground. He was even more surprised to see a familiar face standing guard at the entrance. "Chitto!" he shouted. "Hey, Chitto! It's me, Edward. What are you doing here, old friend?"

Chitto's eyes grew wide and he rushed to Edward. He expertly grabbed the bridle of the horse, bringing the wagon to a halt. In his guttural accent that sounded menacing even when it wasn't, he looked into Edward's face. "Hello, Edward, and goodbye. This is not a good time to be here."

"Now wait a minute, Chitto," Edward said calmly. "I've been welcomed, I've been ignored, I've even been laughed at, but never chased away before. And just who are you to be the one trying to do the chasing?"

Chitto was equally calm. "I am the captain of the Four Mothers Society lighthorse," he said. His eyes locked on Edward, looking for even a hint of disrespect, but Edward just whistled in surprise.

Chitto went on, "And I am not chasing you away. You have the right to be here, just as everybody else. But your arrival is ill-timed. Please come back tomorrow. The powwow will still be going on, although I doubt if you will find many people wanting to partake of your evil census."

"'Evil' is it?" Edward said, his voice rising. "Is it evil to count ourselves and show our strength? Is it evil to show the white man that we can be trusted? Is it evil to—" He stopped in mid-sentence as one flap of the field tent was thrown back. Out stepped Bonaparte, whom Edward had seen only once yet instantly recognized. But it was the tall man behind Bonaparte emerging from the tent's shadow that fascinated Edward.

Standing in his white turban and beribboned long shirt, squinting into the sun, was Chief Isparhecher.

"This isn't right," Edward muttered to himself, turning his wagon. "I think I understand now, Chitto. Perhaps I will see you tomorrow when I return."

"Probably not," said Chitto. "Goodbye, Edward."

CHAPTER EIGHTEEN

Entering the newspaper with a robust flourish, as had become his custom, Edward was met with a sea of faces. "What is this?" he asked. "A meeting of the census team without me?" He laughed. "Maud, please tell me. Is this a plot?"

Indian agent Clem Burton, Benjamin, Tom, and Maud were hunkered over a large roll of muslin-backed paper, with Miss Thompson in feigned indifference a few feet away. The roll of paper went from one end of the display case to the other. It was cross-hatched with little boxes, and circles and arrows were everywhere. It looked like nothing Edward had ever seen.

Benjamin came around the display case and placed his arm easily on Edward's shoulder. He laughed, too. "Now don't go sounding like Isparhecher, finding plots and blackguards behind every tree. This isn't a plot, son. It's a plat. You are looking at Okmulgee. The Indian Commission survey teams have finished their work at last and this is the result." He swung his arm in an arc. "Imagine. Every single town in Indian Territory laid out in perfect grids, north and south, east and west. No more scattershot Indian towns like the old days. See here?" He pointed. "That's Main Street. And that? That's Clem's office and this newspaper. I tell you Edward, old Isparhecher is wrong. There are some things white people just naturally do better than Indians, and making maps is one of them."

Edward said to Tom Sixkiller, "You'll never guess who I ran into last week. Chitto."

Tom was so surprised to hear the name that he missed the trace of bitterness in Edward's voice. "Chitto? What's that scallywag up to?"

"Oh, he just so happens to be the captain of the Four Mothers lighthorsemen now. Our old friend chased me away from a Four Mothers Society powwow up in Okfuskee." He cut his eyes toward Benjamin. "And Father, you believe me to be imagining plots? I found him guarding a tent that was clearly the site of a secret meeting between that Bonaparte fellow and none other than old Isparhecher himself. They were hatching something."

"Rascals all," Tom spat. "So Chitto is now the captain of a toothless lighthorse, of an equally-toothless mob of dreamers preparing to fight the last war. He had a habit of growling to scare people; did he growl at you?"

"Not at all. He was courteous, but insistent. But Captain, he's changed somehow. They say Isparhecher is against allotments because of the money; he will lose most of his leases. But you can see in Chitto's eyes, there is something else. Stopping allotments has become a ... religion to him. It consumes him. I believe he's ready to die for it."

"Or kill?" interjected Miss Thompson.

"Indians don't kill Indians," Tom said flatly and with finality. "Now Ben, tell me how this town grid works. Are you saying that if I had just waited for my allotment, I could have owned a quarter section of Okmulgee rather than a farm I've never seen?"

"No, not at all," Clem said. "Of course, you didn't have

much choice, because the town grids weren't ready, but those of you who took voluntary allotments early got the pick of the litter, as they say. You got 160 acres of good farmland. But now people like Benjamin here can choose between town or farm." To Edward, the latecomer, he explained, "The Department of Indian Affairs is trying to make things fair to the rest, so they're offering the option of two town lots or one quarter section of farmland."

Looking at the map, Benjamin wrote figures in a small notebook. "Of course, it will take the wisdom of Solomon to determine fair value on a land that has never been valued before. It's anybody's guess."

"Yes, but guess we will," Clem said. "And our best guess right now is that an allotment is worth three hundred dollars. If that proves too low, as I am certain that it will be, the Secretary of the Interior has been authorized $560,000 by Congress to make adjustments and reparations. This will take years, but we intend to make it right."

"Three hundred dollars is a lot of money," said Miss Thompson.

"It is, but it is a once-in-a-lifetime payment," Benjamin said. "If you sell your headright, or squander it, there will be no more. To misquote that American statesman and my namesake, Benjamin Franklin: we Indians have been accustomed to hanging together, now we will be forced to hang separately. It's going to be a cold winter for some, I fear."

Edward smiled at his father and pointed to the newspaper office on the grid. "With your permission, sir, I think I'll file for this lot right here."

"I like the way you think, son, but you are a little late to the dance. I printed and backed this map myself. Walked it over to Clem early this morning. See that red dot? That's me. And I put my mark on the house, too. But nice try, mister lawyer. You and yours will always be welcome guests at the Perryman place."

It would come to be known as an Indian summer, but that late September day in 1898 was just hot. Maud had packed a cold lunch of baked beans, deviled eggs and ham to share with Edward. Eating together was a daily occurrence now that Edward had come in from the field.

The census was complete, or as complete as it would ever be. True to his prediction, Monday Grayson had wrapped up his freedmen census, handed it over to Tom Sixkiller with a wink and a nod, and returned to Ft. Gibson to open a general store. Tom, Edward and Maud, with the volunteer help from Miss Thompson, began the tedious—and believed to be completely unnecessary—chore of merging the current census with the old Creek census of 1892. This was a surprising mandate written into the Curtis Act, because the 1892 census had been deemed "unreliable and very probably corrupt" by the Secretary of the Interior only two years before. "Congress wants Indian handprints on it," Benjamin said, "so it doesn't look like it was stuffed down our throats by Old Man Dawes. Everyone knows it was stuffed down our throats by Congress."

Maud and Edward had found a leafy and secluded spot where the sycamores bent over the creek. As she spread the blanket, she said, "You know, back in Ohio we would call this a brook. Creek sounds a bit unrefined to our ear, I guess."

"Unrefined. That's us in a nutshell," Edward said lazily. "I'd like to come to Ohio someday. I'd like to go to Cleveland. The biggest city I've ever seen is Little Rock. Have you ever been to Cleveland?"

"Yes I have, and Chicago as well. Great iron things full of bustle and flow. They are fun for a while, museums and shows, but I couldn't make a steady meal of them. I have simpler tastes." She smiled and winked. "More unrefined, perhaps."

Playing with a deviled egg to avoid eye contact, Edward asked, again too casually, "So what do you plan to do when our work is finished here? Return to 'missionary meadows?'"

Maud smiled, charmed by his boyish subterfuge. "No, I've turned the page on that chapter. Return to Kendall College, I suppose. I've taken a shine to Indian Territory and all things Creek." Her cheeks reddened despite herself. *I'm as hopeless as he is*, she thought. *So this is love. Ye gods.* "What about you, Edward?" She had wanted to say "darling," but lost her nerve. "Going back to Arkansas to practice law?"

"I'm glad you are staying. I'm staying, too," he said.

"Will there be enough legal work to keep you busy?" Maud was setting a trap.

Edward laughed. "Plenty of work, but not much money, I'm afraid. I don't want to work for the Office of Indian Affairs or the commission, and the very thought of working for the railroads revolts me; so I'll be representing other Indians, a proud but poorly-paying profession."

Snap. "Why don't you come teach at Kendall? You could practice law and teach at the same time. I know the college would be delighted to have a lawyer on its faculty. It doesn't pay much, either, but between the two…."

Edward took Maud's now-trembling hands in his and stared deeply into cornflowers. "Miss Fisher, are you proposing marriage?"

Her reservoir of strength completely drained, Maud began to babble. "Was I? Proposing? Well, I can see … in a way … I have never done this before, of course … perhaps I was … suggesting, not proposing…."

Edward gently placed two fingers on Maud's lips. "Let me take it from here. Maud Fisher, will you be my wedded wife for as long as we both shall live?"

"Yes," she said and giggled. "You've got deviled egg on your fingers."

CHAPTER NINETEEN

Maud took the train back to Dayton to tell her father of the marriage. "Are you afraid?" asked Edward.

"Not at all," she said and kissed his cheek. "In fact, he may applaud my ... missionary zeal. Besides, what's the worst he can do? Banish me to live among the heathens? I'm way ahead of him there. Got my own heathen lawyer to prove it."

With his census work done, Edward pitched in to help Benjamin put out the paper. Just like the old days, they'd wrap up the printing Friday afternoon, then retire to the Calico for celebratory steaks and to speak of manly things.

"Ever drink beer?" Edward asked, cutting into his steak. Edward preferred his meat very well-done, approaching shoe leather both in texture and taste.

"A few times," Benjamin said. "Mostly choc. Doesn't hold a candle to cold buttermilk in my estimation. You?"

"No. Maud has, and she says it tastes like bad breath."

"You sure struck gold with that woman, son. Hold on to her tight. Have you two set the date yet?"

"April, if I can stand to wait that long. She'll be staying in Dayton, doing womanly things, building her ... what's the word ... true so? *Trousseau?* I'll be sitting here, running errands for

Miss Thompson and biting my nails. Funny, I never thought about getting married until last month, and now I can't think of anything else."

"Have patience, son. There is world enough and time. And these are about to be your times, yours and Maud's.

"I kind of got the feeling from Captain Tom and Chitto and his Mothers that time isn't on our side," Edward said.

"That's what every generation says: the next one is going to hell. But your future will be bright. Just different. We Indians will have a new place in the firmament." Benjamin fiddled with his glasses, thinking out loud. "You know, in some ways our tribes are like the tribes of Israel back in olden days. They lost their land, just as we have lost ours. But they kept their pride, they held dear their culture, their beliefs, even their language. For a thousand years wherever they wandered over the earth, they carried their nation on their backs. The Jews have proved that land isn't the only thing that makes a people great. They shape whatever land they are on. Perhaps with people like you and Maud, we can become an Indian diaspora, bound together by culture and history, influencing the white culture, taking the best it has to offer and giving the best of ourselves."

Benjamin paused. "Speaking of lost land, do you remember James Bigheart?"

"Sure," Edward said. "He's the editor of the newspaper up in Pawhuska, right?"

"Yes, the *Herald*. Editor, publisher and janitor, just like me. He's a very good man, and a very good friend. And now he has a new job: he's just been elected chief of the Osage. You want to talk about land troubles? They've got it in spades. James inherited a mess and he needs some help." He looked down at his empty coffee cup. "I saw him last week at the press association meeting in Tulsa and … well, proud papa and everything, I started telling him about you passing the Arkansas bar. I thought he was going to jump up and kiss me." Benjamin deepened his voice in what Edward assumed was an impression of James Bigheart and said, "'Oh brother, do we need a lawyer, and now here's an Indian lawyer. And he's your son. I think I died and went to heaven.'" Benjamin chuckled and explained, "Like most Osage, James is a Catholic."

Edward leaned forward, interested. "But if the Osage need a lawyer, why doesn't Mister Bigheart hire an Osage lawyer?"

"For the simple reason that there aren't any," Benjamin said. "The Osage Nation is small, fewer than 5,000 members. Their land problems are far different than ours, but just as compelling. They need a lawyer, son, and James Bigheart would like to talk with *you*. Are you ready for your first paying job? Beats running errands for Miss Thompson."

The mood inside Isparhecher's office was as gloomy as the brown and wet late afternoon that signaled early winter in the Territory. A kerosene lamp on the desk offered only weak light and threw shadows around the occupants, casting them like peasants in old Dutch paintings.

"I can do no more," the old chief grumbled. "You know I did my best, throwing rocks into the road, throwing logs into the stream. But it is over for me now. The people hate me, they have thrown me into the ditch. Pleasant Porter stands on my throat. Soon I will be given 160 acres just like Little Crow who cleans the stable. A chief should be treated with more respect. Did you know I once had grazing rights to more than a thousand acres?" He waggled his finger at Chitto and raised his voice. "And I shared those grazing fees with my people,

Benjamin Perryman be damned."

Chitto didn't know one way or the other and didn't care. To him it seemed that Isparhecher was always talking about changing the color of yesterday's sunset. Chitto's world had no room for yesterdays and scant room for tomorrows. He lived in the present, which made him as innocent as an animal and just as dangerous. He jumped excitedly from his chair.

"We can't give up now," he shouted, turning to Bonaparte, who was staring at the floor. "It's not over. We must honor our ancestors. The land belongs to us all, just like the air and the water." He pointed accusingly at Bonaparte. "You told me you have lawyers in Washington, getting our old treaties back. You told me."

"*Had* lawyers, Chitto. Not anymore. Every time we turn around, another law is passed in Congress that makes our mountain just that much higher to climb. Our coffers are almost empty. Donations have dried up now that the Choctaws and Chickasaws have signed the general allotment treaty. The Seminoles have signed it, too." He exhaled slowly. "The rolls are complete. And the white man is clever. He has put a dollar value on our headrights and let it be known to all. Greed has done the rest. That is all; the dam has burst. We are finished."

Tears of anger streamed down Chitto's face. He pointed with his thumb at Isparhecher. "I expected this old man to fail me, but not you. Not you. You dishonor me. You may be finished, but I am not." He pulled his Bowie knife out of its sheath and held it aloft. "You say the rolls are finished. Well, I know where they are. No rolls, no allotments. You could not stop them, so I will steal them. In the name of my clan, I will. I will reach my father's boat at last. And I will carry precious cargo." Chitto turned and rushed out of the room.

Both men sat stunned. Finally, Isparhecher spoke softly.

"So it seems the snake has gone crazy."

Bonaparte shook his head. "Gone stupid, too. He never was bright, but this is low. Chitto must think that the only ledgers of the rolls are in Muskogee. Poor bastard. There are at least a dozen copies now, with the originals sitting in the office of the Secretary of the Interior in Washington. A fool on a fool's mission."

CHAPTER TWENTY

The Dawes Commission headquarters in Muskogee was a curious and, everybody agreed, singularly ugly building on main street. A three-story clapboard monstrosity that once had been a boardinghouse, it was the only building of large size available in that boom town. It had no electricity, no indoor toilets, and its unpainted latticed porches looked more suited to a gothic novel than a government office.

What it did have was people, hundreds of people every day. Lawyers, applicants, harried office workers, swindlers, and land agents prowled the floors insisting, cajoling, shouting, pleading, waving papers, some just standing in stunned silence as lives were reckoned, often with as much accuracy as the toss of a coin.

Indians crowded the first floor where the ledgers were kept. When their names were found, either on the rolls Tom and his team had compiled or on the highly unreliable rolls from 1896 or 1892, they were issued a certificate of citizenship and sent to the second floor to select their 160 acres. Those whose names could not be found were sent to the third floor to petition for inclusion on the rolls. Maybe one in three, usually full-bloods who spoke only Creek and to white eyes looked obviously

Indian, were added to the rolls. The others, even a few town chiefs, were told no, but that they could appeal the decision at the courthouse across town. The waiting period for a court date was six months and growing.

Every day for a week, Chitto sat in the Embassy Hotel across the street, sipping coffee, watching the comings and goings and planning his attack. Each afternoon around closing time, when the commission offices seemed the most frantic, he would slip unnoticed among the crowd, trying to figure how to do the most damage. He could tell by the pervasive smells of sadness and confusion that he was doing the right thing for his people. He would succeed, he would be exonerated, he would be a hero.

One day it dawned on him: he didn't have to steal the rolls. He would burn down the building.

It was a good idea in theory. The old building looked like it was built out of kindling, the fire station was two blocks away, and the only water on site came from a manual pump out back.

Chitto hit on a plan that he would hide in the large broom closet on the second floor, wait until the place cleared out, and then, under cover of darkness, set fire to the maps, plats, files and papers. He would then go to the first floor in case the fire didn't do the job, take one of the ledger books that had grown in his mind into a living enemy, and escape out the back door without showing himself on main street.

He bought a large box of kitchen matches, stole some greasy rags to act as accelerant, and then late one afternoon in February, 1899, slipped into the broom closet and waited.

Chitto was used to waiting. It was part of being a lighthorseman. He knew that minutes could seem like hours in the boredom of a stakeout, so he waited until the building got perfectly quiet and then waited some more. He fashioned a torch out of the greasy rags and a broom handle, lit it and silently stepped out of the closet door.

Only to discover that he wasn't alone after all. Across the room, assistant land agent Joshua Riddle was quietly committing his own crime: changing allotment records, assigning juicy town plots to himself under two different names and three to his brother John (or Jake, or Jack).

"Jesus, Mary and Joseph," the agent screamed when he saw the torch. He drew a pistol from his desk drawer with surprising speed. "Don't move a muscle. How long have you been here? What did you see?" He paused. "Wait a minute." Riddle's eyes narrowed as his thoughts moved from fear to understanding. "What in the hell are you doing with that torch? I know … you are one of those 'disruptors.' They warned me about you. Told me to keep a gun handy. Get the hell out of here."

Chitto was never good at thinking on his feet, and changing plans in mid-stream was simply beyond him. "I must do this for my people," he growled and stepped toward the other man.

Riddle's eyes widened in alarm and he fired twice. Riddle's first shot tore a chunk out of Chitto's scalp; not a mortal wound, but—like all head wounds—it gushed blood, sending warm rivulets down Chitto's face. The second bullet smashed into Chitto's left shoulder, breaking his clavicle and rendering his arm useless. The torch flew out of his hand and skittered harmlessly into the center of the room.

The shot to his shoulder had made Chitto spin away, and when he came about full circle, the human Chitto had disappeared, replaced by the red-toothed beast that had always lived deep inside him. His Bowie knife had appeared in his right hand, and Chitto sprang into long, graceful cat-like leaps and buried his weapon hilt-deep into the other man's chest. Riddle didn't have time to make a sound, just looked surprised as he discharged two more shots into the floor and died.

Bleeding profusely, Chitto bolted down the stairs, sheathed his knife, and grabbed a ledger book with his good hand. He could hear the yelling out front. "Gunshots!" "They came from the Dawes headquarters!" Holding the blood-stained ledger tight against his chest, Chitto mounted his pony and disappeared into the night.

Disruptor, the wounded beast thought. *I like that.*

CHAPTER TWENTY-ONE

Looking down on the tree-lined streets of Pawhuska, Edward was reminded of something his father told his cronies at the barber shop.

"So, boys," Benjamin had said. "Here's the difference. A rich Indian will build his house in a pleasant spot near the river. A rich white man will change the course of the river to run by his house."

Clem hooted. "If I ever meet a rich Indian, I'll ask him."

In February 1899 Pawhuska was a curious mix, an Indian town laid out on a white man's grid. There weren't any rich Indians in Pawhuska … yet.

In fact, as Edward entered town, it looked shabby and unfinished. Off the main street, trees lined platted streets that barely existed—an abandoned house with cattle grazing in the front yard, a newly-constructed building with piles of bricks waiting to be laid, a sign proudly claiming to be the corner of Elm and B Streets standing in a field of blue stem. Someone had made big plans for Pawhuska … and then ran away to join the circus, perhaps.

The newspaper was reliably familiar-looking, however. Stepping into the *Herald*, Edward could have found the job press, the Linotype, even the coffee pot with his eyes closed. It even smelled the same: that universal tangy perfume of hot lead, printer's ink and paper. It was the Linotype, of course, that forced the design. Everything else hung off that cantankerous, clanking collection of metal like baubles on a mobile. Edward half-guessed that someone fifty years ago in Chicago or Pittsburgh or London had looked around a brand-new print shop, put his hand on the Linotype and said, That's it, you can't improve on perfection.

The only thing different about the *Herald* was the giant who was tossing headline type blocks back into their wooden boxes. Almost seven feet tall, with a shock of white hair that made him look taller, stood James Bigheart.

The Osage were the tallest of all the Indian tribes, and perhaps the fittest. Six feet tall women and six-and-a-half feet tall men were common. When the artist George Catlin first spied them in 1835 in their original home in the Missouri Valley, he proclaimed them "the finest example of physical beauty, Indian or white, I have ever seen." He spent much of his life painting Osage chiefs and warriors.

The Osage were Plains Indians, with far less historic contact with the white man than any of the Five Civilized Tribes. What little contact they had was ambiguous. Bought out of their reservation in Kansas before the Civil War, and forced onto a smaller reservation in Indian Territory, the Osage were justifiably wary when the Curtis Act wrapped all the Plains Indians up in land allotments, too.

The Osage were ignorant of land management, acquisition, sales, leases, and contracts. But as Edward remembered Benjamin saying (probably quoting somebody), "The first stage of wisdom is understanding the depth of your ignorance." The Osage understood and eagerly sought help. Enter Edward Perryman.

James Bigheart smiled broadly and pointed his pica pole at Edward like the tip of a lance. "Don't tell me. You look so much alike, you must be the son of Benjamin Perryman. The young lawyer we have waited for, who will lead my people into the sunshine." He laughed. "And you blush like a white man."

Edward joined the big man in laughter. "Maybe I have much to blush about. Yes, Mr. Bigheart, I am Edward Perryman, and yes, a *young* lawyer. So don't expect miracles from me just yet." He strode forward. "I hope you haven't been waiting long."

"A hundred years. Come in, come in and have a seat." Bigheart placed a hand on Edward's shoulder, a gesture in lieu of the white man's custom of shaking hands, then led the younger man to a chair. Bigheart sat across from him, and his face grew serious. "I hope you don't mind me teasing you a bit. In good times one should laugh. In bad times one should laugh uproariously."

Edward saw his father in this man, and wanted to please him. "Are these good times or are they bad times, sir?"

Bigheart sat heavily in his swivel chair and motioned for Edward to take a seat opposite him. "Depends on who you are, where you are standing, and the time of day, I think. Besides being chief, I am the mayor, for what that's worth. Well, I know what that's worth—a dollar a year. But good times, bad times...." His demeanor turned serious. "Five years ago, the federal government offered to buy our reservation. We said we wanted to think about it. There were smiles all over the room. They said sure, think about it, but remember you can't sell it to anybody else and you will sell it to us. And to show our good faith we will give you ten percent of our offered price each year for five years while you make up your minds. A month later, the tribe got a draw-down from the federal treasury for $20,000.

Those were good times. Everybody got a little money, we built a brick factory, a cotton mill, and brought in lumber for a courthouse and a school.

"I was second chief then, and because I read and write English, I was named representative to the Office of Indian Affairs. They kept asking, 'Have you made up your mind? Have you made up your mind?' Then we were told that because of *their* bad times, Congress was cutting the payment to $10,000. That was a not such a good time for us. Then last year they said no more payments until you sign the agreement. So this is a very bad time for us. That's why you see lumber laying all over the place. You probably thought our town carpenter had died." Bigheart laughed.

Edward leaned forward. "Do you mind telling me how much the federal government offered you?"

"Twenty cents an acre."

"Mr. Bigheart, that is highway robbery."

"You see, Edward, you are already earning your legal fees—even before we have established your legal fees ... or whether you will even take the job as our counsel. But I think you will." He slapped his thighs and stood. "Why don't we walk while we talk?"

Like most Indian towns, Pawhuska was built along a river, adding credence to Benjamin Perryman's joke. The Bird River was chocolate and pretty, a "year-rounder" that never went dry. The railroad passed by the northern edge of town, close to the river, grateful for the abundant water to fuel its engines. Chief Bigheart and Edward sauntered along the often-imaginary streets to the new Harvey House, a hotel near the station.

Edward was a relatively tall man, but as they walked he found himself looking up at a man a full head taller. He wished they had remained seated back at the newspaper, where the disparity in size wasn't so noticeable, but he had a hunch that was exactly why they were walking. He said, "My father told me that your nation's problems were different than the Creeks, but just as complex. Why exactly do you need a lawyer, Chief?"

"Well, our problems are maybe not so much *different* from the Creeks … more like they're inside out," Bigheart said. "Just like every Indian problem these days, it involves land. But here's where the Osage are different. See this street we are walking on? We own it. We own every bit of land for as far as you can see in any direction. And we don't own it by tradition or even by treaty. We *bought* it, lock, stock and barrel. More than a million acres."

Edward was flabbergasted. "But that must have cost a fortune. No disrespect intended, but where did a small Plains Indian tribe find the money for such a purchase?"

They arrived at a set of rattan rocking chairs on the large front porch of the Harvey House. "Good question," Bigheart said, as he took a seat and began rocking slowly, "and you need to know a little history for everything to make sense. You see, the Five Civilized Tribes may be the *biggest* thumb in the eye of the federals, but they're not the only one."

Edward sat quietly, grateful for the opportunity to once again be more or less at eye level with the chief. The latter continued, "Back more than a hundred years ago, long before I was born, the white man was worried about us Plains Indians. We followed the buffalo from Texas to Canada; we wintered where small game was abundant, but rarely in the same place; we came and went as we pleased. The white man, stuck to the land as usual, simply couldn't have us roaming all over the place, so he created prisons he called reservations and put us on them." He smiled. "I'm getting to my point, Edward, just give me time. Anyway, most of those reservations were up in the

Dakotas where white men didn't want to go. They chased us Osage out of the Missouri Valley to a reservation in Kansas, which looked about as wind-blown and barren as the other reservations. But—surprise!—fifty years later Kansas turned out to be the greatest place to grow wheat in the world. Well, it wouldn't do for a blanket Indian to be sitting on land like that.

"So in 1847 we were told to pack up and move to a new reservation in Indian Territory, where all of us Indians could live together and stay out of the white man's hair. No, I'm not making a scalping joke, although lately...." Bigheart laughed robustly.

He continued, "Times had changed by 1847. Jackson was no longer president and the terrible stories of the Trail of Tears and other atrocities against the Indian were well-known and front page on many eastern newspapers. For a short period of time white America seemed to take pity on us. Some Congressmen wanted to make amends, so they passed a law saying they would actually pay us to move here. They offered us twenty cents an acre, and now you know how that figure came up. Charlie Chouteau, our chief at the time, was part French and had lived among the white man. He said, 'Yes we will move, but it will be the last time. You want us to act like white men, we will act like white men. We will buy this reservation, just like white men.' So he took the money we got for the Kansas reservation and bought this smaller piece of land for thirty cents an acre, making Congress feel relieved and sharp at the same time."

He leaned forward and put a hand on Edward's arm. "That ought to be a happy ending, but of course it isn't. Never is with the white man. And now our problems are what you might call eminent. And we need legal counsel. Right now."

Edward studied Bigheart, wondering whether the man had

mistakenly used the wrong word. "Did you mean *imminent*, or did you say *eminent* on purpose?"

Bigheart sighed. "You got me. I was making a bitter joke. The white government is threatening us with eminent domain. I assume, then, you know what that is?"

"Yes, Chief, I do and it cannot possibly apply here," he said, a note of assurance in his voice.

"Why do you say so?"

"Eminent domain is very rare. It's a way for the government—federal, state or local—to confiscate property, and it's damn hard to accomplish. The government has to go to court and prove that the property at issue is essential to the completion of a project, like a bridge or a highway. It's a long and messy process, and in your case, borders on the stupid. How could the federal government claim that your reservation land is essential when there are literally millions of acres on all sides of you that are exactly alike? It's a tactic, Chief, just beating a drum. They threaten you with eminent domain, hoping you will cave in to their offer. This is just bullying. By God, you do need legal counsel and I want to be it."

"I was hoping you would say that," Bigheart said. "Then it is done. If you want to write up some white man papers, I do not mind. I understand we live in two worlds these days. But come inside with me. There is a man in the hotel who has been waiting two days to meet you, although he does not know it yet."

The fern-laden front room of the Harvey House served as both lobby and restaurant. The famous Harvey girls, in their starched aprons and caps, flitted from table to table pouring coffee and refilling baskets of fresh biscuits. Edward was surprised to see that the room was half-filled with traveling salesmen, known as drummers, who dipped into town, hit the general stores and millinery, and would be gone again on tomorrow's train. There wasn't an Indian in the entire hotel, as far as Edward could see. Two worlds indeed.

Seated alone, at a table by the front window, was a well-dressed middle-aged man who wore a trim mustache that was much in fashion at the turn of the century. He rose courteously as the two men approached.

"Chief Bigheart, thank you for coming." He looked to Edward. "I don't believe I've had the pleasure, sir."

Chief Bigheart rested his hand on Edward's shoulder. "This is Edward Perryman, legal counsel of the Osage Nation."

The man smiled, eyeing Edward with real interest. "I was unaware the Osage had legal counsel, sir. How do you do?" He held out his hand and Edward took it.

"It is a recent appointment," Edward deadpanned. "And you are...?"

"Henry Foster, sir, originally of Titusville, Pennsylvania and most recently of Russell, Kansas. It is an honor. Please sit down, gentlemen. Can I interest you in some coffee and biscuits?"

"You sure can," Bigheart answered with his amiable country candor. "I've been smelling those biscuits for half an hour." He slathered one with butter and devoured it in two bites. "Edward, Mister Foster, true to the white man's creed, is interested in our land."

"Well, Mister Foster, you've picked a bad time, I'm afraid," Edward said, vamping. "The Osage are currently in negotiations with the Department of the Interior over the sale of our land. The United States government has informed us that we must sell our land, but only to them. They are also threatening eminent domain, so even the well-known practice of leasing grazing rights could stir sentiments against us. It's all very complicated." Edward wasn't sure just how complicated, but was running out of facts to espouse.

Henry Foster leaned back in his chair with an air of relaxation that surprised Edward. He looked at Bigheart first. "Chief, I want neither your land, nor what grows on it. I want what's under it." He took a sip of coffee, obviously enjoying the moment, then turned his gaze—and explanation—to Edward. "You see, my brothers and I, first in Pennsylvania and last year in Kansas, have been successful in drilling for oil. Oil is the new coal, gentlemen. Oil for kerosene, oil for industry, hell, oil for medicinal ointments; people can't get enough of it. It is the future. And it is far easier to extract if you know where to find it. I have reason to believe that the topographic and geographic features of your land are similar to the Russell fields. I'm a betting man—all oil men are I suppose—and I am willing to bet on your reservation holding oil. It's betting on a three-card flush, I admit, but if we hit, the Osage and my company will be splitting a mighty big pot. What do you say? Will you lease me your mineral rights? We'll pay three cents an acre."

Bigheart took another hearty bite of biscuit, signaling Edward to do the talking.

"Mister Foster, that is an interesting and wholly unexpected offer," Edward said. "We will, of course, need to review how this will have an impact on our ongoing negotiations with the Department of the Interior, as well as review your offer when it is presented in writing."

"You'll have it," Foster said eagerly. "But tell me: am I in the running? Have you leased your mineral rights to anyone else?"

Edward gave a sideways glance to Bigheart, who was still playing dumb by examining a fern. "You are in the running,

Mister Foster," Edward said. "We will expect to see your written proposal delivered to Chief Bigheart at his newspaper within one month. Good day, sir, and thank you for your interest."

"Thank you," Foster said, and handed Edward one of his business cards. "If anything should change, please contact me first."

"Certainly."

As the two Indians headed back to the newspaper, Edward let out a long whistling breath, a sigh of relief. "Chief, you know I was fishing without a hook back there. It sounds good, but I have no idea if the Osage even hold the mineral rights to your land. Do you?"

The giant Indian clapped his hands in delight. "Hell if I know. Check with my legal counsel."

CHAPTER TWENTY-TWO

Slipping in and out of consciousness, Chitto knew it was only a matter of time, perhaps minutes, before they would be after him. He had entered the white man's world, killed one, and stolen one of their precious books. He would be hunted.

And in his fevered mind his hunter had a face: Tom Sixkiller. Chitto believed Captain Sixkiller had gone over to the other side, doing the devil's work to complete the census. He would come looking for his book.

Chitto also knew that even though no white man could catch him, Tom Sixkiller could. Tom taught Chitto how to track, and would use those skills against him. The captain knew his haunts, knew where he was born, had been to his cabin. Chitto couldn't go back to his familiar hills.

The captain would catch him and kill him. Or worse: make him rot in prison.

So Chitto turned his pony to the south, into Choctaw country. Perhaps he would find some people from the Four Mothers Society he could stay with while he healed, or who would at least give him medicine and something to eat before sending him on his way. Or maybe he would find an abandoned cabin or a cave. Yes, a cave. He'd put his bloody book deep in a cave and guard it like a wounded she-bear.

He rode all night in the kind of trot his pony could sustain for days as long as they had water. Chitto didn't know exactly where he was, but he could figure that out later.

Dawn found him on the crest of a hill, looking into a small valley. Despite his weakness, Chitto was struck by the beauty of the locale. This would be a good place to die, if it came to that. Descending to the valley floor, he spotted a rough-hewn cabin among the trees. There was no smoke coming from the chimney, but Chitto gingerly dismounted, took cover, and waited for signs of life. He put himself into a hunter's trance. Even delirious with pain, he could send his mind away like a mountain lion waiting out his prey while his eyes kept vigil.

Finally, about midday his horse started grazing toward the cabin. At least the pony felt safe. Weakened by loss of blood, Chitto decided to take a chance and crawled up behind the cabin. The place was silent. Chitto was aware that abandoned cabins were ordinary these days. Those damned allotments were almost never in the same location as homesteads, so people simply took off to find their new 160-acre headrights. Rough and unsteady cabins such as this one would be easy to abandon in the best of times, but to Chitto it looked like salvation.

He crept around the corner and, to his delight, found a large earthen pot filled with hominy in briny water, steeping to become *sofki*. With his good hand he pulled a handful of hominy out of the pot and wolfed it down. There was enough here to last him for days, if he lived that long. He waited a few more minutes, then crawl-walked into the empty cabin, lifted himself onto a plank bed in the corner, and fell asleep.

Chitto awoke in a panic. He felt tied down. Looming above him was a man staring intently into his face. Maybe he was still hallucinating. "Captain, don't!" he screamed and reached for his pistol. But it was gone, along with his bloody clothes. Blankets covered him, and when he struggled to rise, a fiery pain stabbed him in what he saw was his now-bandaged shoulder.

"Be still," the man said in Choctaw, then he repeated in English. "Be still." Recognizing a flicker in Chitto's eyes, he continued in broken English. "You be good. You safe. Fever gone." He patted Chitto lightly on the chest. "Sleep again. Then we eat." He put his fingers to his mouth.

When Chitto awoke a second time, the man had become smaller and younger. "Leave me!" Chitto yelled. "Are you a devil? Why do you change shapes? Let me be!"

"Change shapes?" The young man laughed. "Oh, you think I am my father. We mean you no harm. We know who you are, and we are happy you live. I am Jumper Maytubby, son of John Maytubby. You are the lighthorseman of the Four Mothers, called Chitto. I am glad you feel better." He patted Chitto's leg under the blanket.

Chitto squinted. Through a dry mouth he asked, "How long have I been here? Where are we? How do you know me?"

The young man, Jumper, laughed again. "Questions, so many questions. Am I back in the academy?" He handed Chitto a cup of water. "You have been here for four days, maybe five. I found you," he said proudly. "Well, actually, I found your horse. She led me back to you. Father and I cleaned you up and we took out the bullet."

Jumper opened the cabin door and gestured to someone outside. His father entered and nodded courteously toward Chitto. The older man held the blood-stained ledger in front of him like an offering.

Chitto stared at the book. "How did you—? I'm sorry. I am

confused. Thank you. Thank you for caring for me. Where did you say I am?"

"You are in a cabin a few miles from our town, Tamaha," Jumper said.

"Tamaha," the father repeated and said something in Choctaw. His son said, "My father says you will like Tamaha. No railroads, no telegraphs, no white men, no troubles. Can you eat?" He lifted a gourd bowl of *sofki* from the floor and placed it near Chitto's lips.

Chitto felt that his body had passed beyond hunger, but he took a few sips, more out of courtesy than need. Now that he was fully awake, he had also passed through fear, leaving only curiosity. "So how do you know me? Did we meet at a Four Mothers powwow?"

"Four Mothers," the father said, nodding his head and moving his hand palm down in a circular motion.

"Yes, my father said he saw you often. But everybody knows you now. You killed the white agent, you took the book. You are a famous Indian. The white man has posters everywhere wanting you. They will pay fifty dollars."

Chitto was alert now, yet completely at peace. He spoke softly. "So is that why you are keeping me alive? To get the money?"

The older man clearly understood more English than he could speak. "No money!" he said roughly. "No money. You fight. You fight white man, you beat white man. You Crazy Snake. You leader now." He made another circle with his hand.

In response to Chitto's confused expression, Jumper explained, "That's what your people are calling you now: Crazy Snake. Fearless in battle. We are through with Bonaparte. He wanted to talk with white men. You know better, because you know what the white man understands. He doesn't respect us.

So you say fine, then you can fear us instead. We are few, but we are ready to follow you."

Chitto laid back and closed his eyes. *Harjo*: fearless, or crazy, in battle. *Chitto Harjo*: Crazy Snake. He liked that even better than Disruptor. Perhaps it would be good to die another day.

CHAPTER TWENTY-THREE

Edward needed to find evidence that the Osage owned mineral rights to their million-acre reservation, and he hoped to find that evidence in the 1847 contract of sale between the federal government and the Charlie Chouteau-led Osage.

Knowing his own tribe's casual disregard for the preservation of all written contracts and treaties, Edward wondered where, or even if, he would find one for the Osage. Time meant different things to Indians and whites, and fifty years in Indian time was measured in song and stories told by grandmothers. Edward had learned with the census that paper trails were impossible to establish because, with no written language, Indians had no use for paper until recently.

Edward was standing beside James Bigheart in the newspaper office as the chief, now in newspaperman mode, was working the job press treadle with his foot. Meanwhile Edward fed sheets of paper onto the platen, just as he had done a hundred times for his father. "Chief, if we are going to legally enter into an oil exploration lease with Henry Foster, I need to know if there is anything in writing that can prove the Nation's authority over mineral rights. The answer may well be in the 1847 sales contract. Do you have a copy?"

Bigheart shook his head. "No, it got burned up during the war, probably to start a fire to keep my people warm. But I know a place where you can find every treaty, every contract, every broken promise. Have you ever known a white man to throw away a piece of paper? I haven't seen the place, but I am sure the contract is stored at the main Office of Indian Affairs over at Ft. Smith. I'll be willing to send a telegram introducing you as Osage legal counsel and tell them to let you see everything."

The Office of Indian Affairs in Ft. Smith housed the archives of every document pertaining to every tribe and band in Indian Territory, recorded and filed by tribe and year. The archives were so large, they occupied their own two story building.

Edward approached a heavyset woman at the reception desk. A wooden sign on her desk said she was Mrs. Baker, and she was making marks in the front of a book. Flanking her at drawing tables were four men transcribing ledgers. The large room was so quiet, Edward could hear the scratching of the pens.

"Good morning," he said brightly in a voice that echoed through the stacks. "My goodness," he said a good bit softer, "it's quiet as a tomb in here."

The woman giggled. "You should be here when we are fully staffed. It gets to be as noisy as a library. How may I help you?"

"Ma'am, I am Edward Perryman, legal counsel to the Osage Nation. I have come to review old treaties and contracts between our Nation and the federal government."

"Yes, Mister Perryman; we received a telegram from your chief. Welcome. Would you like any assistance?"

"No, thank you. I know what I need, if you would not mind

just pointing me in the right direction."

"It's just as well." She giggled again. "I'm going to be up to my neck interviewing for new scriveners. I have five slots open, if you can believe that."

Edward could see no reason not to believe her. "Is that what those gentlemen are doing?"

"Yes, we are copying every single document in this building and sending them to Washington for safekeeping. It has become a matter of some urgency, I'm afraid."

"Why is that?" He made a show of looking around. "This place seems safe enough."

Mrs. Baker's voice became a conspiratorial whisper. "I'm sure that's what the folks at the Ardmore office thought, too, until the fire."

"Fire?"

"Yes, they burned the building down and everything that was in it. They say it was that villain Chitto Harjo and his gang. Thank goodness it was at night so nobody was injured."

"Chitto *Harjo*?" Edward asked. "Did they destroy the Dawes rolls?" He felt surprisingly proprietary.

"Well, yes, I suppose everything burned in the fire. But the rolls had been copied in triplicate months ago. Not so with all the active documents and assignments, all the proof of citizenship papers, all the plats and maps. Up in smoke." She made a motion with her fingers like smoke dissipating in thin air. "Ardmore is our southern office, responsible for the Chickasaw, Comanche, Caddo, and Lord knows how many other tribes. It's going to take months to piece things back together."

Seeing Edward's raised eyebrows, she added, "Don't worry, Mister Perryman. The Osage papers have already been transcribed." She coughed apologetically as she consulted a grid on her desk. "It's not such a big tribe, you know. You will find everything you need in aisle CC, shelves two and three." She pointed with her pencil. "That's in the northeast corner over there."

"CC, shelves two and three," Edward repeated to himself as he walked into the stacks. His right and left brains were in conflict. Logically, he knew that the governmental juggernaut would eventually have its way with allotments. The die was cast. Wasn't that why he was here, to find a way to survive within the new system? But his romantic right brain couldn't help admiring Chitto for raging against the night. Both Chitto's crusade, and very probably Chitto himself, were doomed. Edward thought that would not bother his former lighthorseman companion; he might find the lost cause aspect of his tiny war one of its attractive features. He had earned his new name: *harjo*, crazy in battle, fighting against the odds.

The librarian was right, the Osage shelves were only half full. Edward found the 1847 contract almost immediately, in a file box labeled 1840-1850. There were also a slew of letters between Chief Chouteau and Secretary of the Interior Pierce that indicated negotiations went smoothly between the two nations. Edward was impressed with the chief's command of English and frontier sense of humor. The letters from the secretary were dry as dust and were probably written by a factotum, but Chouteau's were chatty and funny in the deprecating humor of the day. He called the new reservation "our little piece of the great earth," a curious term for more than a million acres. Perhaps only a Plains Indian, used to roaming from Texas to Canada, would have such an expansive view. Edward wished he had known him.

The contract was precisely as Edward had expected: boilerplate upon bull manure upon heaping portions of boredom.

There was no mention of mineral rights one way or the other. It probably hadn't occurred to either side. Even the coal deposits found in the Cherokee lands near the Arkansas border hadn't been discovered until after the Civil War.

But there was a provision in the contract that Edward had not seen in his law books. It said that the land described in the contract would be "under the sovereign control of the Osage Nation, all of whose constitution, amendments and laws are incorporated by reference." Now where was that constitution?

On the next shelf, as it turned out. Chief Bigheart was right. Maybe the white man didn't always honor his promises, but he sure kept track of them.

Edward recognized the Osage constitution immediately as being a version of the Cherokee constitution, which served as the basis for the Creek, Choctaw and Chickasaw constitutions as well. But like all governing documents, the Osage constitution was a living document capable of change, and it was in the third amendment, dated July 2, 1884, that Edward hit pay dirt. It listed and described the duties of the various Osage councils. There was the fish and game council, which controlled fishing and hunting on the reservation; the cattle council that authorized tribal representatives to enter into grazing leases; and the mineral council, which authorized the leasing for extraction of all underground material, "including, but not limited to gold, precious gems, coal, oil and gas."

Edward closed the big book, stopped by Mrs. Baker's desk, paid ten dollars to order a transcript of the constitution, and walked out the door whistling.

♦ ♦ ♦

"Well, Chief Bigheart," Edward said at the Pawhuska newspaper the next day, "you are in business. Your authority to lease drilling rights to Henry Foster or anybody else is spelled out in your constitution. But please do me a favor: Henry Foster has already waited months for this. Let him wait another month. I need to go to Ohio to get married."

CHAPTER TWENTY-FOUR

James Bigheart pushed his way into the front office of Benjamin Perryman's newspaper. The Creek editor, his reading glasses slipped to the end of his nose, had been peering over Miss Thompson's shoulder as they edited the want ads.

Without raising his head, he glanced over his eyeglasses at the newcomer. "Well, if it isn't Jim Bigheart," Benjamin said. "Come to see what a real newspaper looks like? And I'll save you the asking: no, this beauty is not for sale."

The big man laughed. "I wouldn't take it as an ante." He strolled over and heartily clapped a hand on Benjamin's shoulder. "Hello, old friend. I came to see my legal counsel, formerly known as your son," Bigheart said. "Seen him around?"

"He's in the back getting some of that witch's brew Miss Thompson calls coffee." Benjamin pretended to dodge a tender punch to his arm. "Edward," he called, "you've got company. Come out with your hands up."

"Hello, chief," Edward said, strolling to the desk that once served as Maud's Dawes Commission headquarters. "You caught me just in time. Another three days and I'd be on my way to Ohio." He put his cup down on the edge of the desk and gave Bigheart a flinty look. "Okmulgee is a little far for you to travel for a simple visit, isn't it? Is something wrong? Please say no, I'm getting married next month."

"I'm not sure, Edward, that's what I need you to tell me," Bigheart said. He pulled an envelope from his coat pocket. "That Foster person may be a good oil man, but he's no good at keeping secrets. Apparently, he told somebody he was going to sign a lease to explore for oil on our reservation, and that somebody told somebody else, who told the Indian Affairs office, who told the Secretary of the Interior, who sent me this letter." He waved it in the air, almost ready to crumple it in his large hand. "I'm not clear on everything it says, I'm no lawyer, but what I do understand angers me, Edward. It talks to me like a child. Respect is not a river, it is a road."

"Except when that road passes through Indian Territory, it seems," Edward said. He held out his hand for the letter. "May I?"

Edward sat at the desk, all the better to examine the contents. In a few moments he looked up, fire in his eyes. "What an insult, Chief Bigheart. He condescendingly calls our government 'Great Father.' You have every right to be angry. It says that while the sale and redistribution of your land is pending, you may do nothing to encumber, modify or diminish its value." He looked at the chief. "The Department has no such authority. Bad law, bad precedents, bad manners." Edward returned his gaze to the letter. "It also demands you go to Washington to appear before an officer of the Department, to show cause why you are hindering the government's generous offer. And it threatens eminent domain. Outrageous." He again looked at Bigheart. "Are you going?"

Bigheart nodded toward Benjamin. "I can't, Edward. Just like Ben, I have a newspaper to put out. Besides, I am so mad, I just might choke the 'Great Father' if I have a chance. But I've got another idea. We Osage will be happy to pay for you to take a trip to wherever you choose if you will first make a visit to Washington on our behalf. Consider it a wedding gift?"

The meeting between Edward and Deputy Assistant Secretary of the Interior Raymond Clifton started badly.

Edward was already a little cranky after a train ride that took three days, involved five changes, and promised far more adventure than it delivered. Even though the man at the desk at the Willard Hotel gave him detailed instructions, he still got lost and arrived at Mister Clifton's office ten minutes late. He knocked respectfully on the opaque glass door.

"It's open," came a voice from within.

Edward walked in and stood awkwardly in front of a fat man reading papers. Finally, after the longest three seconds Edward had ever experienced, the man, without rising, barked, "Who are you? Are you my ten o'clock? I was expecting an Indian."

Edward's eyes narrowed. "I am an Indian, sir. Edward Perryman, legal counsel to the Osage nation."

"You don't look like an Indian."

"What are we supposed to look like?" Edward asked with deadly calm. "Oh, you mean my headdress? It's back at the hotel with my law books."

"Late and impertinent, too. This should be interesting," Clifton grunted. "Let's hope you read those law books, Mister Perry, because you are going to need them. You and your little band of Indians are standing in the way of American progress and you shall step aside, sir, you shall step aside."

"It's Perryman, Mister Clifton, and do you think it possible we can have a conversation without threats and recriminations filling every sentence? May I sit down?" He didn't wait for an answer, but selected a chair facing the desk. His posture was bolt upright.

Clifton leaned forward, crossing and uncrossing his chubby fingers. Then he tapped his palms lightly on his desk and regarded Edward with sad, heavy-lidded eyes. "You are right," he said softly. "I am sorry. I'm tired; I'm just so tired. You may not know it, but from my perch up here in Washington, working with you Indians is like grabbing smoke." He paused, but Edward did not do anything to fill the silence, so the man continued. "You don't trust us, I know that. You have reason not to. But there's nothing I can do about the past. All you and I have to work with, Mister Perryman, is tomorrow. And tomorrow is built on shifting sands."

He waggled a finger for emphasis. "Let me give you an example: we are on the brink of an agreement with the Cherokees, say, and a month later we are told those were the wrong Cherokees, or the old Cherokees, and the new Cherokees need time to study and talk over the agreement, maybe a long time. It drives me crazy."

Edward nodded and smiled. "Yes, our ways can seem mysterious to whites, just as yours befuddle us. I can remember, when I worked with the Dawes Commission, the mistakes that were made. Indian agents—who, by the way, were never Indians—came into our Creek towns looking for the town chief. They invariably found one, because we have many. Our chiefs are more like congressmen than presidents, equals with an equal voice, and able to act only with a majority. Just like your Congress, that takes a bit of talking, and the wheels turn slowly. The Indian agents think they know us, but they don't. They keep thinking chief means king. Did you know that most tribes elect their chiefs, just as you do your congressmen, and we can get rid of them just as fast?"

Clifton smiled as well. "No, I did not, and that explains a few things. How would you like a job in Washington?"

"Wild horses, as they say," Edward answered amiably. "But if you would like to come to Indian Territory, I'll teach you to ride a horse—one that's gentle. And I'll feed you chicken and dumplings that are so good people write songs about them."

"Tempting," Clifton said. "But you'd need a pretty damn big horse, I'm afraid. And there's still this little matter of selling us your land. Talk about befuddling, Mr. Perryman. Here we are, willing to pay you good money for your land and then give it back to you, free and clear, 160 acres at a time, to each and every member of your tribe in general allotments." He offered his hands in a bowl to Edward like Oliver Twist asking for more porridge. "What could be fairer than that?"

"Quite a few things, in fact. The Osage nation...."

"See, right there," Clifton interrupted, pointing his finger. "Osage nation. I know something about your so-called *nation*. I hail from Rutland, Vermont, sir, a farm community. We don't pretend to be any more than that. Yet there are more people in Rutland than live on your entire reservation. Why did you call yourself a nation?"

Edward maintained his calm. Truthfully, he was beginning to enjoy this. He could smell blood. "*We* didn't, Mr. Clifton; you did. The Osage are very intelligent, but, like all Plains Indians, they have no written language. The first use of the term 'nation' was applied to the Osage by the United States government in treaties, and reinforced over the past hundred years. The sovereignty of our nation has now been established by case law and the Osage constitution, which was written by *your* government and forced upon us in 1872. *You* made us a nation, now you must treat us as one."

Clifton had lost his cheerful demeanor. "Nation, tribe, band, it makes no difference. Your tribe is an artifact of the past, I'm afraid. Congress has decreed that the tribal system cannot be sustained in our modern America. Little pockets of sovereignty will not stand, Mr. Perryman. We fought a great civil war to insure we are one nation indivisible. The Osage live in America, and are obliged to acknowledge and obey the laws of America. Will you obey our laws, sir?"

"Will you acknowledge and obey your own?" Edward pulled a letter from his suit pocket. "This letter from Secretary of the Interior Pierce to Osage Chief James Bigheart threatens eminent domain against his reservation unless a sale is completed immediately. Aside from being preposterous on its face, the United States Constitution—*your* Constitution—forbids the application of eminent domain by the government without due process under the fifth amendment and just compensation under the fourteenth amendment. The Osage have been offered neither due process nor just compensation. You stand in violation of the Constitution, Mr. Clifton." Remembering Chief Bigheart's words, he added, "The law is a road, not a river."

Clifton took the letter from Edward's hands and sighed deeply. "I wrote this letter, as you may have guessed. It was just saber rattling, which happens often enough. All right, Mr. Perryman, what will it take to effect a sale of your reservation land that is both lawful and beneficial to both of our governments?"

Edward hesitated. He was pretending to gather his thoughts, but he had been thinking about little else since he boarded the first train in Tulsa. "Well, I believe it would be in everyone's best interest if we were afforded a hearing before the senate committee chaired by Senator Pettigrew." Edward smiled. "He is one of the men who created this mare's nest, after all. We want an open and fair hearing, Mr. Clifton. That is all we are asking."

Clifton smiled. "Mare's nest, scorpion pit, fifth level of hell. That chicken and dumplings is sounding better by the minute. Thank you for your time, Mr. Perryman. You are a worthy representative of the Indian people. I'll see what I can do."

CHAPTER TWENTY-FIVE

Tidy.

A curious word for Edward to use, and maybe he had never used it before, but it was the only word he could think of to describe Dayton, Ohio. Lawns, which were unheard of in Indian Territory, were everywhere, edged in boxwood hedges and flower beds; neatly trimmed carpets of green laid in front of freshly-painted front porches. Many of the streets were black-topped or oiled, with fire hydrants discretely placed a few paces from each corner. Edward harked back to Pawhuska's Street Signs to Nowhere and marveled.

Edward had stumbled into a white man's Eden, and he liked it. Maud, who seemed perfect to him in Okmulgee, now radiated a graceful beauty he had not seen before, like a gem in a proper setting. Maud's willingness to give this up to teach Indian children in schools with outhouses and no running water touched Edward deeply.

Maud's father, Reverend Fisher, had secured a room for Edward at the Young Men's Christian Association, which overlooked the Main Street bridge. Edward's room was as tidy as the town itself, and superior to the lighthorsemen bunkhouse he had once called home. The Main Street trolley would take

Edward within three blocks of Reverend Fisher's home, but Edward was filled with curiosity and preferred to walk those spring mornings and evenings. As he traveled along the unfamiliar sidewalks, he felt very cosmopolitan.

Edward had been to a circus in Little Rock, and except for elephants and tigers, Dayton provided a similar cavalcade of wonders: horse-drawn trolleys, street lamps, bathtubs, lights that went on and off by pushing a button. Downstairs at the YMCA there was even a crank telephone that was constantly in use by the residents. Edward envied them because he did not know anyone on earth he could call. Maud said her father refused to install a telephone because it would be used only for frivolities and gossip. When Maud suggested that it might be nice to have one in case of emergencies, Reverend Fisher said that Dr. Bacon lived only three doors down, and if the Lord wanted him sooner than that, he was ready to meet his maker.

Reverend Martin Luther Fisher had been on Edward's mind for some time. He had conjured a mental image of Maud's father that proved surprisingly accurate. In Edward's mind, the Reverend was short. He was; Maud had him by a good two inches. Edward had seen him as thin. He was, but sinewy and electric with vitality. Edward had seen him as bald, and again he'd hit the mark. This last may have seemed prescient, but in fact wasn't. Indians, full bloods at least, carry a fortunate genetic trait that precludes baldness. There are no bald Indians. So Edward often thought of white men, especially those in powerful positions, as bald. It made them less intimidating, cut them down to size, like Samson shorn of his locks.

And Reverend Fisher could seem intimidating, at least at first blush. He was taciturn, and used his calm silences as a weapon. Edward could see how this might unnerve the gregarious Maud and keep members of Fisher's congregation in thrall. But the silence and stares had no effect on Edward whatsoever. As an Indian, he was used to them and, in fact, expected such behavior from his elders. He would say his piece to the Reverend, nod his head in respect, and wait.

If there was a surprised member of this pas de deux, it was Martin Fisher. The other young men who had come to call on Maud had talked too much, fawned too much, sweated too much, bragged too much, so much that Fisher tolerated them only as far as he felt his Christian courtesy demanded. This suitor was different. He absorbed Fisher's steely glare like a champion boxer absorbs a blow; he listened, really listened. And when he spoke, he had something to say. Fisher was fascinated, and by the second afternoon, the two men could be found drinking iced tea (a novelty for Edward) and chatting on the front porch. Fisher peppered Edward with questions about growing up Creek, about Benjamin and his newspaper, about life in the saddle as a lighthorseman, and what the future held for Indian Territory.

Maud was flabbergasted. "My father adores you, Edward. I better hurry and marry you before he attempts to adopt you." She grinned impishly. "Of course, Father always said his best times were spent among the aborigines. This just proves it, I guess."

In the days leading up to the wedding, Edward and Maud settled into a satisfying routine. After a breakfast at the YMCA cafeteria, Edward would amble the few blocks to the Fisher house. Most mornings Maud would play the piano—Chopin, Beethoven, Liszt, pieces that he had never heard before, but were oddly familiar, and enchanting. Edward made a silent pledge that even if he were to spend the rest of his days barefoot, his wife would have a piano.

Maud and Edward would take long luncheon strolls along the banks of the Great Miami River or in spotless parks with benches and fountains. They ate very little, held hands like children, and talked deeply about their future together—which would begin in less than a week.

Their discussions of life were the only times that Edward felt wisps of uncertainty float through his mind. His entire past, present, and future were rooted in Indian Territory. But did Dayton run through Maud's veins the way the Creek nation ran through his? Would she tire of Indian Territory, and consequently of him? Could a white woman raised among such luxuries remain happy to live forever in the relatively backwater lands of Oklahoma? As usual, he decided to sidle up to the subject.

"You know," he said, finishing his apple and throwing the core into the river, "this is a mighty fine city. If you would prefer to live here in Dayton, why I could—"

Maud placed her finger gently on Edward's lips. "Now see here, Mister Perryman. You don't have enough words in that lovely vocabulary of yours to talk me out of Indian Territory. I thought this conversation might come up; to be honest, I've had similar conversations with myself over the last few months. Here's what I decided.

"Yes, Dayton can be pretty." She gave him that throaty laugh. "Well, except in February and August, when the Devil runs roughshod. And I'll always be grateful for my safe and secure childhood here." She smiled dreamily, as if catching a glimpse of her past. "Dayton is a fine town, darling. But like so many things in this world, perhaps its strength is also its weakness. I am not seeking safe and secure. I don't know,

Edward, perhaps I inherited it from my mother, but I have an unquiet heart. My father went to the Belgian Congo out of religious purpose; my mother went out of love and curiosity. I possess both in abundance.

"I didn't stumble onto Indian Territory, I was drawn there. And just as I dreamed, I found in you, your father, so many others, a thirst to be part of the future; part of an uncertain future made of mud, sticks, sweat, and determination. You may be too close to see it, but you are building a new state out of whole cloth. Speaking on behalf of our future children, we want to be part of that. Will you marry me, Edward? My imaginary children need a father."

Edward laughed and held Maud close. "Saturday can't come soon enough, my love." Then he grew serious and turned his eyes to the river. "Funny you would mention mud. According to the stories of the Creek people, in the beginning there was only mud, and we rose from it. Perhaps we are about to start the Perryman creation story."

When Maud and Edward returned to the Fisher home, they found the Reverend at his writing desk, pen racing across paper, eyes burning, jaws clamped. Edward had seen his father in a similar mood when he wrote his scorched-earth editorials, and knew to remain quiet. Maud, of course, plowed straight ahead, ignoring the fearful angels on her way.

"Heavens, Father, you look like a man possessed." Only half in jest, she added, "I can only hope and pray you are not writing our marriage vows."

Martin Fisher dropped his pen abruptly and slicked back his few remaining wisps of hair. He smiled, although his eyes still smoldered. "I'm sorry, children. I was totally absorbed in a most disturbing sermon. Perhaps I should save it for another day." Now his smile was sincere, even loving. "But I must earn my daily bread. After I pronounce you man and wife and send you off to years of wedded bliss, I must return to the pulpit and tend to the souls of my flock." An edge returned to his voice. "And believe me, some in that flock, a few who may well be in attendance next Sunday, need tending badly."

"Why is your sermon disturbing, Reverend?" Edward asked.

Fisher gave Edward a grateful nod, then arose and began pacing, his kinetic energy getting the best of him. "I've taken the title of my sermon from Mathew 19, 'Suffer Little Children.' An ambiguous phrase, don't you agree? I first got the idea a month ago, when I read a small piece in the newspaper about a mine cave-in just thirty miles east of here—Xenia mine number four. Three miners were killed. Nothing particularly unusual about a mining disaster, they happen all the time. But near the bottom of the story I read the names of the dead miners. One of them was Wesley Gorham, a name that will be etched upon my soul for the rest of my life." As if his eyes were staring into infinity, he explained, "Wesley Gorham was eleven years old."

Maud gasped, and involuntarily raised her hand to cover her mouth.

"I couldn't believe my eyes," Fisher continued. "I visited the newspaper for confirmation. The editor said yes, it was tragic, but not unusual. Many children work in the mines, he said. Many children work everywhere, he said. You should see the textile factories down south, he said. It would break your heart." He pulled a folded sheet of paper from his vest pocket. "Then he quoted these lines of doggerel:

'The golf links lie so near the mill,
'That almost every day,
'The laboring children can look out,
'And see the men at play.

"It's a poem by a woman named Sarah Norcliffe Cleghorn. I wrote those lines down because I never want to forget them. Like poor Wesley Gorham, they are lodged forever in my heart, like broken glass."

Maud's voice trembled. "Eleven years old. I didn't know, Father. I just had no idea. Aren't there any laws?"

Fisher's jaws tightened again. "To our great national shame, no. Since visiting the newspaper, I've been doing extensive research. Over the years, dozens of groups, including our own Ohio Council of Churches, have pleaded with Congress to enact child labor laws. But these pleas fall on deaf ears. The corporations own this country. They own Congress, bought and paid for. What congressman wants to bite the hand that feeds it? So child labor laws die in committee, while children die in mines and mills. And at least two heads of the largest corporations in this nation will be sitting contentedly in the pews of my church on Sunday, knowing they and their companies are above the law. American corporations can do no wrong." He sat down again, exhausted.

"And they call Indians savages," Edward said, his emotions stirred. "This is an upside-down world, that is certain. Corporations can do whatever they wish, while we, recognized sovereign nations, can do absolutely nothing. Congress treads on us like we were vermin, takes away our governments, our police, our courts; then takes away our farms and homesteads, makes us sign papers of loyalty, and finally gives us back some of the land on an individual basis on the seemingly benign, but entirely sinister, concept of divide and conquer."

Martin Fisher just shook his head ruefully. "We've fallen down the rabbit hole, the Red Queen is now our king, and we must change the color of our roses." He coughed a mirthless laugh. "Perhaps your Indian nations should acknowledge our topsy-turvy country and remake yourselves into corporations, with your tribal members as stockholders. Then nobody could touch you."

Edward and Maud stared at each other in a silence born of enlightenment. Maud nodded her head, answering Edward's unasked question.

Edward smiled. "Reverend Fisher, you may not know it now, but you may have turned tragedy into at least a bit of triumph. You may also have given me a wedding gift that can be shared throughout Indian Territory."

CHAPTER TWENTY-SIX

The nightmares returned to Chitto; vengeful, accusing, relentlessly crying and begging for help. Chitto would thrash, his body stained with a sweat that had an unfamiliar and unpleasant metallic odor. His hair would be wet, his mouth parched.

His waking hours were worse.

Chitto had always been a lone wolf; he sought no one's counsel, and offered none. And now he found himself the accidental leader of a doomed cadre of dreamers, as unprepared for the present as they were vague about the future.

Unlike Shakespeare's boastful Malvolio, however, Chitto had no interest in greatness, thrust upon him or otherwise. But the straggling remnants of the Four Mothers Society decided he would be their leader, and he couldn't shake them.

He had changed during his convalescence. He had chosen the wrong approach. He knew that now. Indian against white man was flea against dog; an annoyance that would soon be accepted as normal. Dawes Commission offices that had once held two clerks now held five men, armed and on alert. His destruction of offices and ledgers had galvanized his enemy, not harmed it.

He saw what he had to do. He may be an accidental leader, but a leader was needed—a leader who would explore a different path.

That path opened to him when he was in Ardmore, waiting for the Indian office to close before he torched it. Two marshals were arguing loudly outside the office.

"I ain't going to do it, Billy. You go out there," one of the men said.

"Not me, pard," said the other. "Remove an old lady from her house because those idgits inside signed her homestead over to somebody else? Can't you just see next week's newspaper? 'Widow driven from home by cruel U.S. marshals.' No thank you."

"You don't know she's a widow," said the first man.

"Oh, hell, all them old Indian women are starving widows when the dang newspapers get through with them."

So they are, thought Chitto, *so they are.*

A few weeks later young Maytubby led Chitto to the first meeting of what would be called the Snakes. They met at the stomp ground in the Creek nation, near the Cherokee border where he first met Bonaparte. Although he saw a few familiar faces among the forty or fifty men assembled, neither Bonaparte nor any of the other original leaders were there. Chitto also saw that the men were mostly either old or very young, and he knew this spelled danger.

Chitto was resigned to die at some point during his war of attrition against the evil allotments. He was, after all, wanted for murder. But he needed assurance that those who insisted on following him knew the consequences. He would speak the truth, even if it left a bitter taste on his tongue, and fear in his listeners.

The men began a low sing-song chant: *Chit-to Har-jo, Chit-to Har-jo, Crazy Snake, Crazy Snake.* It wasn't exactly a name Chitto relished, but he accepted it. Your warrior name wasn't really yours to choose.

He stood on the same flat rock he had seen Bonaparte use as a platform. Because there were at least four tribes represented, he would speak in English. Chitto was well-versed in English, having ridden with the loquacious Jubal for three years and having crossed paths with many whites during his time as a lighthorseman. He could only hope that his audience knew enough English to follow his words.

"Thank you, my brothers, for joining me," he said. "You and I know we are entering upon a journey to save our land, the land that has been ours by treaty, been ours by blood, handed to us by our ancestors. This land is a part of us like the trees are a part of us, the rivers are a part of us," he stamped his foot on the outcropping, "this rock is a part of us. And we are part of it.

"Our journey will not be an easy one. Even if we are successful, we might be killed. If we are unsuccessful we will be ridiculed. But our fathers—John Ross, John Jumper, Motey Tiger, the great Sequoyah—beg us to try."

"Kill the white man," a voice in the back shouted, followed by a scattering of yips in agreement.

Chitto held his hands high. "No, my brothers, that is the road to the edge of darkness. Where we are hundreds, they are thousands. That was my early mistake, a mistake I now admit. Many of you know I served with pride as a lighthorseman of the Muskogee nation, called Creek in English. I faced many a gun barrel and knife point. I fear no man. But bravery—or *harjo*—is not enough.

"I know the white man. He is stupid of our ways, but he is not evil—not all of them.

"But the white man is many, and he believes his papers have power. When we resist his papers, we will do so without further violence. He will be confused. He will send more papers. We will burn them, but still we will not harm him. Then he will send men to throw us off our land, but we will not go. We will stand at the doorway of a homestead and we will ask the newspaper man, 'Does the white man need land so badly he would kill this old woman for her cabin?' And the newspaper will repeat the question for the world to hear.

"Every day, every moon that we resist, will seem like a year to the white man. He is impatient. He will finally see that there is a place for the Indian in his world and that the treaties signed by his fathers were wise. He will agree to go back to those wise treaties, and we will be family again, farming together, hunting together, living together in peace, in peace with the land and in peace with the white man. This is what I say."

Things went well for Chitto and his loose-knit band of confederates at first. He convinced the entire full-blood population of Okfuskee to take their certificates of citizenship, deface them, and send them back in a box to the Indian Agency in Okmulgee. Benjamin Perryman wrote sympathetically about that act of passive resistance.

In May, the Dawes Commission office in Tahlequah mysteriously burned to the ground, but the Tahlequah *Times* was far less than supportive of the Snakes this time, calling the fire an act of vandalism that must be punished. Chitto scolded the leader of that group, saying he was playing into white hands. The young man hung his head like a misbehaving puppy and scuffed his moccasins on the dirt in front of him. And like a puppy, Chitto knew, he was bound to do it again.

Chitto felt like the lead buffalo in a running herd. He remained the leader only so long as he stayed in front. He was bothered by this. With him, their resistance was dangerous, but possible. Without him, the young hotheads would prevail and likely be killed. His nightmares had blood in their mouths.

Taking a page from the Four Mothers, Chitto would hold Snake "councils" adjacent to already-planned ball games, powwows and church camps. This was a not-so-subtle show of force, and many of the full-bloods who had felt abandoned sought Snake protection.

It was at a Creek feast day in late May that the comfort and protection of Chitto and his Snakes reached their height and sowed the seeds of the Snakes' downfall.

George Ijo, who owned a large smokehouse and tannery, approached Chitto in a frenzy, tearing at his shirt and pulling his unbraided hair in the fashion of Indian lamentation. "If the Snakes are to protect us," he shouted, "today is the day and this hour is the hour. Will you come? Will you come? Will they take my wife and children … my wife and children?" He was almost incoherent.

Chitto stood quietly, waiting for more of the story, but the distraught Ijo had roiled the other men. "What is the matter, brother? How can we help?" said the impetuous young Jumper Maytubby, who had more or less appointed himself Chitto's aide-de-camp.

Ijo pointed into the distance, back the way he had come.

"The marshals. Two of them. They are at my front door. They say we have had too much time, they can wait no longer. They say our house does not belong to us. They say they sent many letters from the court and now we must leave with them. I knew you were here. I snuck out a back window. My children … you must help us."

Chitto spoke at last. "Of course, we will stand with you, my brother. Tell me, did you get letters from the court?"

The man wrung his hands in frustration and stared at the ground. "Maybe. I cannot read white man words."

Chitto stiffened. "Maybe these white men will be able to read Indian sign. Get your ponies, men." He pointed to Ijo. "You ride with me. Take us to the back of your house."

Two dozen men got to a copse of scrub oak fifty yards behind Ijo's home and dismounted. Chitto spoke quietly to his men. "Run around to the front of the house and stand arm in arm. Make a wall. Do not let the marshals through. I know them, they won't hurt you. They have orders not to shoot." In a steely tone he emphasized, "But you do the same. Keep your heads about you. Hear me? No rifles, no knives. Not even a rock." He laughed softly. "You listening, Long Deer? Now hurry."

The men laughed as well, glad to relieve the tension. They went tearing around the house to confront the stupefied marshals, who had been smoking cigarettes under a shade tree in front. The Indians were silent. They just locked arms and stared at the lawmen.

"You can't do that," one of the marshals shouted as he stumbled to his feet. His command was met with an ominous high-pitched turkey gobble from in back of the human wall. Spooked and outnumbered ten to one, the marshals grabbed their horses and mounted on the run, their wild-eyed ponies as unnerved as they were. They left a whooping, yipping, and laughing crowd in their wake.

The grateful George Ijo and his wife brought out a large basket of peaches, a platter of smoked meats, and cool pitchers of water. And almost by magic, a brown bottle of whiskey appeared, making the rounds of the happy men. A victory, even one as small as this, over the white man turned the group festive.

For a while.

In less than half an hour, the celebrating men and Chitto saw a cloud of dust that preceded a company of marshals—a dozen men armed to the teeth. They slowly trotted their horses toward the Ijo home with military precision. The Indians reformed, but with less resolve—skittish, looking to each other for support.

A white-haired man incongruously dressed in a fedora, tie, and vest sat like a church deacon on a big palomino. "I am Captain Jacob Webb, United States Marshal, and you are all in violation of federal law," he said. "You will disperse immediately or I am authorized to arrest you for resisting a valid eviction notice. Leave now or I will be forced to remand you to jail."

"Stand your ground," hissed Chitto. "They don't want a fight any more than we do."

He was right, but Webb and his men weren't going anywhere either. The two sides glared at each other, anger mixing with fear.

Then a derisive gobble broke the silence.

"Eat one of these, turkey boy," shouted one of the marshals, and fired a shot that splintered the rough shingles above the Indians' heads.

"No!" yelled their captain. "Cease fire! Cease fire!"

But it was too late. A knot of teenaged Snakes broke away

and rushed the nearest marshal, pulling both rider and horse to the ground. This prompted another marshal to fire into the crowd multiple times. Perhaps he, too, only meant to fire warning shots. But his horse shied, causing him to miss badly, and at such close quarters, two Indians fell.

"Cease fire, goddamn it, cease fire!" screamed the captain. "Oh, dear sweet Jesus, withdraw! Cease fire! Withdraw!"

"Scatter!" Chitto shouted. "Get out of here! Go home and stay there!"

Chitto and Maytubby helped their wounded companions back to the scrub oaks.

He spoke softly to the boy he was holding. "Can you ride, son?"

"I think so," said the boy, who then died in his arms.

By the time the chagrined marshals got back to Muskogee, their collective conscience had reimagined the skirmish in their favor. And Chitto was about to feel the razor-sharp double-edged sword of the press.

In three days, *Harper's Weekly*, followed swiftly by the Eastern newspapers, reported on the Battle of the Smokehouse and the "Indian Uprising" led by the savage renegade Chitto Harjo. Harjo—*Harper's* incorrectly used the term as if it were a white man's surname—had once been a member of "the elite mounted Indian police known as the lighthorsemen."

"Ain't nothing worse than a lawman gone bad," deputy United States Marshal Bass Reeves was quoted as saying. "The sooner these Snakes or whatever they call themselves are brought to justice, the safer our womenfolk will be."

CHAPTER TWENTY-SEVEN

Edward and Maud spent their honeymoon in Chicago, staying at the reliable Harvey House near the Dearborn Station. They walked in wonder among the thousands of tulips in Grant Park and rode the still-novel elevated train that had been built for the Chicago Columbian Exposition a few years earlier. They strolled along Lake Michigan, which took on an oceanic presence to the land-locked Edward. They attended a concert by the brilliant pianist Paderewski (which secretly pleased Edward because he wore his wedding suit, thus assuring at least two wears out of the expensive bit of haberdashery), and dined on unpronounceable dishes in fancy restaurants.

Some days they would end their Grant Park walk with a visit to the new Art Institute, where a stunned Edward would sit for long minutes on a bench facing Seurat's massive *A Sunday at La Grande Jatte*. Edward turned his astonished eyes to Maud. "They say art imitates nature. Not this time. This fellow has found a way to take nature and blow it into a million pieces, then put them back together in tiny stars of color. I see something different every time I come here."

Maud kissed him gently on the check. "Your boyish sense of wonder is one of the main reasons I married you," she said.

"Tell me another reason," he teased.

"I'd prefer to show you back at the hotel," Maud said, then laughed. "Oh, that look is priceless, dear husband, just priceless. Never lose it. Come, I'll race you to the Harvey House."

They also spent hours at the public library, breathing life into Reverend Fisher's idle suggestion. With Maud acting as stenographer and Edward as researcher, they learned about the different types of American corporations, partnerships and trusts; corporate legal restrictions and privileges; the issuance of stocks and bonds; everything they hoped they would need to form the oil and mineral company for the Osage. Maud had even come up with a title for the nascent corporation: the Indian Territory Illuminating Oil Company.

"Building a proper board of directors is going to be key," Edward said, laying his pencil aside. "And it can't be just Indians. Congress will tell us we can't run a corporation just like they say we can't run a nation. I intend to beat them at their own game."

History decided not to wait on the oilman Henry Foster and the Osage nation, and handed the baton of discovery in 1898 to the adventurous George Keeler. Thanks to the same geological savvy as Foster and a bit of wildcatter's luck, a shallow well sunk in the south forty of Josiah Bartle's farm hit sweet crude in monstrous proportions—first the Red Fork, and later the Glenn Pool oil fields. Every oilman in America, including J. Paul Getty and Harry Sinclair, made a beeline for nearby Tulsa, a Creek town lucky enough to be both a railroad hub and sitting on the banks of the mighty Arkansas River. In two years, Tulsa went from a sleepy village to a thriving city of 4,000, with its own seven-story skyscraper, appropriately called the Petroleum Building. Tulsa became known as the Oil Capitol of the World, and the place where Edward Perryman intended to go shopping for board members.

First, though, Edward needed to make a home for Maud and himself. This was going to be a little tricky because if all went well, Edward would be spending time in Pawhuska, Tulsa, and Washington, and Maud didn't know a soul in any of the three towns.

They decided on Okmulgee, at least for a while. Maud knew many of the Okmulgee townsfolk from her year working on the census, and she would be under the protective wing of Benjamin Perryman.

It was Benjamin who came up with an agreeable short-term solution. At his usual post in the newspaper office, he took Maud's hands in his. "Why don't you and Mrs. Thompson live in my house while Edward is gallivanting around, and I'll go sleep at Mrs. Thompson's? I could come over for home-cooked dinners, especially when Mrs. Thompson makes her famous chicken and dumplings. What do you think of that, Mrs. Thompson?"

Enid Thompson flushed, but tried to remain outwardly calm. Secretly she was thrilled. Here was her chance at last to live in Benjamin's house and sleep in Benjamin's bed, though not at the same time as the man himself. "Yes," she said rather shyly, "if that would be satisfactory with you, Maud, I'd be honored."

Later that afternoon, Benjamin and Edward took their usual places on the Perryman porch swing as Benjamin readied a few things in his carpetbag, preparing for the three-block journey.

Edward explained the plan to form a corporation to benefit

the Osage people. Benjamin kept nodding his head in agreement. "That's brilliant, son. By making the tribal members stockholders, you provide Congress with the assurance of individual ownership, while giving the Osage the same collective protection of a corporation that they used to enjoy with the tribe. Can I help?"

"Very much, Father. I need to go to Pawhuska immediately to explain the plan to James Bigheart and then, if he agrees, get approval from the tribal council. Then I need to form a board of directors. I want to form an ironclad board, one that Congress will not only accept, but envy. I would like you to serve on that board, sir, and help me find ways to approach leaders in the oil business, men of vision who will take a chance with us on this venture."

Benjamin smiled proudly. "Why, of course I will participate. And James Bigheart is a noble man who more than lives up to his surname. *And* I know a few other people who can help. But if you really want to get to the inner circle of oilmen, you need to talk with my old friend John Landis. He's the publisher of the *Indian Republican* and knows everybody worth knowing in Tulsa. He's a very good friend of mine, and I know he will help you. This is just the sort of new thinking that will appeal to him." He paused and smiled. "Besides, he kind of owes me a favor."

"What kind of favor?"

Benjamin's eyes danced. "Well, let's just say you shouldn't bring up the press association dinner in Guthrie last year."

Edward grinned. "Only as a last resort, sir."

♦ ♦ ♦

John Landis was a raw-boned, big-knuckled Irishman with a built-in belly laugh. He had the face of a club fighter—which he once was—with a nose permanently pointing to five o'clock. His broad, honest facade revealed a broad, honest disposition. No one could resist his charms, but many had underestimated his journalistic prowess. Some had paid the price. His newspaper, which in a few years would change its name to *The Tulsa World*, was a power in the Territory.

"Welcome, Edward Perryman, welcome," Landis said, walking around his ornate desk to shake Edward's hand. Edward was impressed, semi-awed, by the contrast between his father's office and this one. It was clear that while Benjamin Perryman catered to Indians, this man dealt with oil barons.

Landis led Edward to matching cane-back chairs, sat like a big cat, and tossed off a hearty Gaelic laugh. "Well, I guess your old man has already told you how he saved my ass in Guthrie last winter."

Edward's eyebrows betrayed him. "Um, no details, sir, just that he did."

"Oh, hell, none of that 'sir' shit, Edward. This is a first-name world. That's why I like it. Yes, your father saved old John's ass and reputation at that press association dinner. It was the seventh-most boring dinner of my life, and I'd been taking regular nips of my Irish medicine to brace myself. Which is to say, I was as high as a Georgia pine, three sheets to the wind, aces and eights. After dinner was supposed to come the annual award presentation, and everybody in the room knew it was going to go to Benjamin for his editorials about the Four Mothers Society. But damned if the head of the press association didn't stop by my chair and whisper, 'Get your speech ready, Johnny me boy, you're the winner.'

"Well, your da was sitting near, and when he saw my

glazed eyes, he stood up and literally carried me outside. It was colder than hell; I thought my nose was going to fall off. Benjamin walked me round and around that hotel, talking me through my acceptance speech—which he composed on the spot. I finally sobered up and he brought me back in, just in time to pick up my award." He gave another bubbly laugh. "Some folks say it was the best speech I ever gave." He grew serious. "I owe your father for his generosity and kindness. Now tell me how I can help you."

Edward carefully laid out the unusual situation with the Osage and their ownership of their reservation, the pressure by the federal government to have them hand it over so it could be handed back in shattered pieces, and his plan to create a corporation for oil and mineral rights that would preserve tribal cohesion while honoring the congressional intent for individual allotments.

"The thing that will allow the corporation to be taken seriously," Edward said, "is a board of directors of Indians and whites, the best oil and business minds in the Territory that will convince Congress that we know what we are doing and let us do it."

As Edward was wrapping up, John Landis moved to his desk and started scribbling on a large tablet. His hooded eyes were suddenly charged with energy, locking Edward with a gaze that took no prisoners.

"I have a few questions for you, Perryman," he said at last. "How many Osage are we talking about?"

"It's a small tribe," Edward answered. "2,982 tribal members as of last year's Dawes census."

"Less than three thousand stockholders. That's a manageable number. How do you know there is oil on the reservation?"

"I don't, but Henry Foster thinks there is, and he's willing to pay us three cents an acre lease to find out."

"How many acres?"

"A million."

Landis whistled. "Damn, money is just flying all over the place these days. I know Henry, he's an oilman's oilman. If there is oil there, he'll find it. And I believe he will find it, he knows what he's doing. Hell, Edward, this Glenn Pool field is so damn big it may stretch all the way to Kansas. There's so much of it and it's so shallow, you can damn near stick a straw in the ground and start sucking. But here's the big question: our newspapers are full of stories of unsuspecting Indians selling their headrights for a few dollars or a bottle of whiskey. What's to keep your Indians from selling their stock for pennies on the dollar, and your company winding up being owned by Sooners and scalawags?"

Edward coughed. "To be honest, I don't know. I'm working on it. Do you have any suggestions?"

Landis laid down his pencil. "I may have, and I bet my friend Waite Phillips will know. He's set up a dozen companies."

"You know Waite Phillips?"

"We could be cousins," Landis laughed. "I guess I forgot to mention just how this drunken paddy scribe beat out your father for editor of the year, did I? I wrote a four-part profile, some would say a valentine, of the Phillips brothers—lauding their willingness to risk everything time and again to change the face of the twentieth century and, yes, make themselves rich in the process. And speaking of rich, I think you've come up with something special for the Indians, Edward. I knew somebody finally would, and I couldn't be more pleased. I guarantee you that both Waite and I will serve on your board of directors, and we know four or five more, good men and true, who will join us."

♦ ♦ ♦

After three whirlwind days in boardrooms and oil derrick dog houses, a slightly dazed Edward Perryman returned to Okmulgee with an Indian Territory Illuminating Oil Company board of directors that was not only ironclad but jewel-encrusted.

CHAPTER TWENTY-EIGHT

Chitto, renamed Chitto Harjo, was now the most-wanted outlaw in Indian Territory.

The Eastern press, which had fabricated the "Indian Uprising" out of half-truths and lies, now had a story line to satisfy its racist, morbid fascination with the Indian as a savage who kidnapped women and scalped men. *Harper's* explained away Chitto's non-existent rebels as "elusive" and "cunning," whose "cowardly strikes" must be stopped before all-out war ensued. Crimes all across the Territory, real and imagined, were laid at the feet of the Snakes. Politicians were demanding, as Congressman Mahan from Missouri put it, that this "ruthless band of marauders who prey on innocent government workers" be brought to justice. A $500 reward for Chitto dead or alive was posted by the *Police Gazette*. Deputy United States Marshal Bass Reeves, wearing a paisley cravat and surrounded by a bevy of reporters and photographers, announced that he would lead a specially-deputized posse "to end this murderer's rampages once and for all."

In fact, for almost three weeks since the confrontation at the smokehouse, Chitto and his tiny gang of hangers-on had been on the run. The entire Snakes movement now consisted of young Maytubby, Johnny Nokose, who was a true believer like Chitto, and the Watson twins, who everybody acknowledged were a little slow. Again, Chitto would have preferred to go it alone, but he felt a reluctant loyalty to Maytubby, at least. Even under his leadership, he knew they were likely to die.

But not like this, surely not like this: starving to death? Was there no salvation left in the nation? His own people had turned their backs on him.

Chitto had to use every trick he had ever learned as a lighthorseman to avoid capture. The entire Territory was crawling with marshals and bounty hunters. Even Indians who had once supported the Snakes were turning away in fear. Chitto was confused and hurt, but should have understood. The bounty hunters were little more than outlaws themselves, and to them one Indian looked pretty much like the next. Two Chickasaw men hunting rabbits near Tishomingo were killed by bounty hunters who claimed they were Snakes and had shot first. The judge released them with a lecture on gun safety.

Finally, his men and horses exhausted and close to starvation, Chitto decided to take them to his little cabin and barn hidden in the Creek woods near the Deep Fork of the Canadian River. He knew there was some risk in this, but his cabin had gone undetected many times before. His barn was full of hay and his root cellar was stocked with sweet potatoes, dried corn, even a few cured hams and fatback.

His men stayed in the barn's loft to sleep on the soft, sweet-smelling hay, and Chitto slipped onto his wooden bed in his tiny cabin. But sleep was elusive. His stomach was full, but his soul still hungered.

Drenched with night sweats, Chitto rose around midnight and walked down to the river to sink into the forgiving tepid waters of the Deep Fork. He just drifted with the current, his wounded mind thinking about death. The idea of suicide had no currency with Chitto, but what if he just kept floating? Floating down to the Mississippi, floating out to sea, floating out of this world into the next to fish again with his father?

His body floated on, his mind in this dream-like state, for a mile or so, until he reached some shallows and snagged his long shirt on a partially-submerged branch. *Damn, I can't even do this right,* he thought, and waded back to shore.

Turning toward home, Chitto saw a glow in the sky that he knew could be only one thing. He broke into a run and soon heard the endless crack of gunfire, shouts, and the screams of dying men and horses. His wild-eyed pony, its mane on fire, ran crazily past him and disappeared into the night.

When he arrived on the scene, it was too late. The cacophony of the ambush had been replaced by something far worse: silence. Both the barn and cabin were engulfed in fire. The roof and two walls of the barn had collapsed and blazing bales cascaded from the loft like a river of flames. Everyone was dead. The Snakes were no more.

Chitto had never learned to cry in sadness, if indeed there was learning to it. It didn't matter; no amount of tears could dilute his grief.

Chitto stared at the smoldering remnants of his cabin and barn with lifeless eyes. He sank to the ground and began rocking back and forth in feral moans. But his pain was one no animal had ever experienced—he was ashamed to be alive.

All night he sat rocking and chanting the death songs of the old people, those he could remember. When dawn broke through the blackjacks, he stood. Clad only in a torn and sooty long shirt, he started slowly walking downstream, walking to the Mississippi, walking to the sea.

♦ ♦ ♦

He made it all the way to Okmulgee. It took him three days to cover the thirty miles, which is not bad when you are barefoot, half naked, and avoiding people who are sworn to kill you.

But he needed to get there. He really had no place else to go. Aside from his cabin, the lighthorse bunkhouse in Okmulgee was the only home he knew. He wanted to die a lighthorseman, even if he was the last one. Besides, he had something to say, and Benjamin Perryman was the one man Chitto thought would listen.

Chitto knew where Benjamin lived. He had been there a few times with Captain Sixkiller. And he thought it would be a far safer place for him than the newspaper, which was in the heart of town. He crouched in a thicket behind the house until sunset, then snuck around to the front door. He was greeted by an aroma so wonderful he staggered slightly as he stood on the front porch.

He rapped lightly on the door. In a minute, he came face to face with Enid Thompson, which surprised him and frightened the living hell out of her.

Her gasp was audible. "Chitto, you are supposed to be dead," she said, louder than she intended.

Chitto started backing off the porch, waving his arms like an umpire calling a runner safe. "I won't hurt you, Miss Thompson. I won't hurt you."

Benjamin appeared behind Mrs. Thompson's shoulder. "We know you won't, son. Get in here quickly. Mrs. Thompson, please close the door."

Benjamin grabbed a throw from the sofa, wrapped it over Chitto's shoulders and hustled him into the kitchen.

"May I please have something to eat?" Chitto asked quietly.

"Of course, Chitto," Benjamin said. "Sit down. Dinner's not quite ready, but you can get started on this." He slid a loaf of bread, a crock of butter and a pitcher of buttermilk in front of the hungry man.

"I did not mean to frighten anyone," he said as he began to eat. "I don't expect anyone would believe me, but I swore off violence months ago."

Benjamin took the chair beside Chitto. "Mrs. Thompson wasn't afraid of you, Chitto. She thought she was seeing a ghost. The world thinks you are dead, my friend. Every newspaper in the Territory is reporting that you and your rebel gang were shot or burned to death at a farm west of here. Bass Reeves is taking credit."

Chitto chewed slowly, his throat threatening to close up. "Some gang," he said. "Three men and a boy. They're dead all right, that much is true." His eyes were moist even though his expression was completely stoic. "I should be. I wish I was."

Benjamin patted him on the shoulder. "Don't talk like that. You are a brave fellow. You have been a staunch defender of traditional tribal ways. I don't agree with your methods, but you have spoken well for a way of life. It's not your fault that what you say falls on deaf ears."

"That's why I'm here, Mister Perryman. I want to speak one last time. I want to say my piece in your newspaper."

"We'll get to that in time," Benjamin said. "But first things first. No offense, Chitto, but you don't smell so good. Go out back and wash up. We are about the same size. I'll bring you some pants, a shirt and an old pair of boots. Then we can dig into Mrs. Thompson's lamb stew."

Chitto returned looking like a preacher or maybe a banker. Like most men of the time, Benjamin only had four shirts, and two were dirty. Chitto was wearing what Benjamin called his "Sunday-go-to-meeting" shirt.

"You look very handsome, Mr. Chitto," Mrs. Thompson said approvingly as she laid down steaming bowls of stew.

"Thank you, ma'am. I'm all dressed up for my own funeral," he said with something that approached a chuckle.

"Let's talk about that," Benjamin said thoughtfully. "The way I look at it, if you want to stay alive, you're going to have to stay dead. The white press re-invented you into this great Indian menace, and now with bugles blowing and flags flying, they killed you off. They did you a favor, son. Staying dead is probably the only chance you got of getting out alive."

"How can I be dead in Okmulgee? Everybody in town knows me."

"What about Mister Sixkiller?" Mrs. Thompson said. "Could he help?"

"Oh, that's brilliant, Enid," Benjamin laughed, oblivious to the wide-eyed astonishment of his co-worker. To the best of her memory, outside of introductions, this was the first time he had called her by her first name in conversation.

"The Captain? Is he still around? I'm confused," Chitto said, shaking his head.

Benjamin stared at his crossed fingers which he had formed into a steeple. "He may just outlive us all. I got a letter some time ago dictated by my dear friend and your old boss Tom Sixkiller, from the King Ranch down in south Texas. He's been hired on, along with a bunch of other ex-lawmen—Texas Rangers and such—as border patrol to keep Mexican bandits on their side of the border. He says the pay is pretty good and the food isn't half bad. He asked me if I knew of any old lighthorsemen looking for work. I'd forgotten about the letter until right now. How would you like to be dead in Brownsville?"

"I think I would like that very much. But I don't have any idea how I'd get down there…."

"You can't wait, son. You are on borrowed time here. You should leave tonight." Benjamin spread his fingers wide. "I'll lend you my horse and a few bucks. You can pay me back later."

Chitto nodded. "But before I go anywhere, I still want to speak my piece. I have to."

"Let me do that for you," Benjamin said. "Tell me what to say."

The two men talked deep into the night.

CHAPTER TWENTY-NINE

Through his connections with John Landis, Waite Phillips and other members of the board of the Indian Territory Illuminating Oil Company, Edward quickly developed a list of clients. In addition, the Caddo tribe near Anadarko, with a reservation structure similar to the Osage, asked Edward to be its legal counsel. But it was Maud and her music that cast the deciding vote to settle in Tulsa.

She had been sitting at her old desk in Benjamin's newspaper office, writing up the official notices while Edward sat idly by, drinking coffee. Mrs. Thompson crossed the room and handed Maud an envelope. "It's for you, dear," she said.

"You've got mail?" Edward asked with raised eyebrows. "How did anybody know you were here?"

"It's from Kendall College," she said, turning the envelope over in her hands without opening it. "When we were at Wheaten, I asked my old faculty advisor to see if there were any openings at Kendall. I knew we were coming back to the Territory, though I didn't know where; but I know we've been talking about Tulsa lately, not Muskogee. Think I should open it anyway?"

"Why, of course," Edward said. "Nothing is set in stone."

Maud sliced the envelope open and read silently for a few moments. She then turned her eyes up to Edward. "Well, as my father would say, 'The Lord moves in mysterious ways his wonders to perform.' The president of Kendall says that this will be the final year for the college in Muskogee. The school will close for a year, then merge with the Tulsa Conservatory and re-open as the University of Tulsa. The president says if I can wait a year, he'd like me to join him on the faculty of the university's new music school." She smiled broadly. "What do you think?"

"I think we are on our way to Tulsee Town. Congratulations, my dear Maud."

They found a small house just two blocks off the river, then returned to Okmulgee to pack Maud's trousseau and Edward's books and clothes.

Waiting for him at the office was a telegram from James Bigheart: "Come to Pawhuska. Senate committee orders you to Washington in two weeks."

Edward grabbed his wife around the waist. "My friend Raymond came through as he said he would," he said happily. "Although I can't say much about his timing. But this is our big chance, Maud. The future of the Osage nation and the new corporation you named hang in the balance." He raised his voice and looked across the office. "Mrs. Thompson, would you mind having a roommate for a few more weeks?"

Upon Edward's return to Pawhuska he reported to James

Bigheart. The amiable, easy-going giant was leaning his massive frame against the heavy Washington flat-bed press in the middle of his newspaper pressroom. He clapped a hand on Edward's shoulder. "Edward, the council and I have every faith that you will succeed on our behalf in Washington. Your work for us has been outstanding. To show our appreciation, the council has voted you a full share in the corporation. The stockholders now consist of 2,982 Osage and one Creek.

"The council figured, quite rightly I believe, that if you prevail, we will all be rich together; and if you fail, we will all have empty bellies. Good luck, my friend."

Raymond Clifton met Edward in the hall outside the senate hearing room. The rotund man led Edward to one of the long benches that lined the wall.

"Senator Pettigrew will be chairing the committee and asking most of the questions," Clifton said. "You have nothing to fear with him. He will very likely admire you, in fact. He likes brains. Just don't say anything negative about general allotments. That was his idea as much as anybody's, and despite its rocky start, he still believes deeply that individual ownership of land is best for the Indian and best for this country. I'm not asking you to praise the issue of headrights. I know you have too much integrity to do that." He checked his pocket watch, really just a dilatory tactic to give him time to choose the right words. "I'm just suggesting you be, how should I put it, nimble. Dance around it; please don't plow into it head first."

He checked his notes. "Senator Landreneau of Louisiana will also be there. He often looks asleep, but he's not. He's sharp. Let's see. There's Senator Thaddaeus Peabody of my home state of Vermont. He often looks awake, but he's not. He's a mean-spirited, irritable old fart who left his brains in the maple shack. Just say yes sir and no sir like you would to a rich uncle at Christmastime. And remember, it's not you; he doesn't like anybody. The hearing is open, so there may be a few more senators dropping in. The subject matter may be of real interest, especially in California and Texas. Have you ever testified before?"

Edward shook his head. "First time, and I'd be lying if I didn't say I have butterflies." It wasn't the fear of speaking in public, or of possibly arguing with powerful senators, that made him nervous; he knew he was a good speaker and a quick thinker, and he knew the subject matter. No, it was the fear of failing the Osage who were laying all their hopes on his shoulders. Almost three thousand lives resting on a single man.

"You certainly handled yourself with me. Too damn well, if you ask me." Clifton laughed. "You shouldn't have a problem. But you may feel insulted. Aides, assistants, pages, secretaries, hell, janitors come and go in these meetings like they own the place. You are just another stranger to them and they can be downright rude at times, shuffling papers and reaching across the table just as you are making your most important point. There is not a damned thing you can do about it, but forewarned is forearmed. I'll be in the room the whole time, and I may toss you an easy question from time to time if I see members losing interest or you get in trouble." Edward smiled appreciatively. "Ready?" Clifton asked.

Edward clapped his palms on his thighs. "As I'll ever be."

◆ ◆ ◆

Testimony before the United States Senate Committee on Indian Affairs, Honorable Richard Pettigrew presiding.

Senator Pettigrew: The chair recognizes Edward Perryman. Mr. Perryman, the Secretary of the Interior has asked this committee to clarify whether it was congressional intent to include mineral rights in Indian general allotments. Are you here representing the Indians?

Mr. Perryman: No, Senator. I am here representing the Osage.

Senator Peabody: What's the difference?

Mr. Perryman: That is a good question, Senator. Thank you for asking. "Indian" is a convenience term in the English language used to describe a group of people, just as the words "European" or "Oriental." Although we never use it, we don't object to the word "Indian," any more than a Swede or Italian would object to "European." But a Swede is not an Italian, any more than a Choctaw is a Navaho. Thank you for allowing me to explain.

Senator Peabody: Seems like splitting hairs. [laugh] But please don't split mine. I'm still wearing it.

Senator Pettigrew: [aside] Please, Thaddaeus. [pause] Mr. Perryman, I have here a lengthy and quite thoughtful analysis of the Osage historical relationship with the United States prepared by Assistant Secretary of the Interior Raymond Clifton, present. He makes a persuasive case that through treaty, contract, and constitutional agreement, the mineral rights of the Osage are in evidence. Although I am convinced that most of the language addressing mineral rights was borrowed from other documents, I acknowledge the paper's persuasiveness. What I will not, and never will acknowledge, however, is any attempt to undermine or in any way weaken the spirit or the letter of the general allotment acts of 1895 and 1897. My colleagues in the field, Senator Dawes, Senator Curtis, and I have spent many years crafting legislation that assures every American—Indian and non-Indian alike—the opportunity to participate equally in this great nation. The American way of life that rewards individual achievement—whether on the farm, the frontier, or in a workshop in Menlo Park, New Jersey—is precisely what has made our nation the greatest in the world. Now I ask you, sir. Isn't giving valuable mineral rights to an Indian tribe flying in the face of individual freedom? Are you not asking us to support an antiquated village system of government that cannot be taken to scale?

Mister Perryman: No, Senator. We understand and embrace the pillars of American democracy. In fact, what we are proposing is at the very heart of our mighty nation: the American corporation. As you know, our corporate laws provide individuals the ability to join in common cause when the task is too large for any one person to accomplish. United States Steel, the mighty Grace Steamship Company, Indian Territory's very own Phillips Petroleum Company, are the future of America. We know this. That is why we have formed the Indian Territory Illuminating Oil Company, and ask congressional approval to transfer Osage mineral rights to that corporation.

Sen. Pettigrew: What relationship would members of the Osage tribe have with this company?

Mr. Perryman: Each member of the nation will be issued one share of stock in the new corporation.

Senator Peabody: What do savages know about running a corporation?

Mr. Perryman: I would assume nothing, Senator. If I should ever run into a savage, I will suggest he change his career objectives. [laughter] I ask at this time that Mr. Clifton be allowed to distribute the names and affiliations of the members of the board of directors of the Illuminating Oil Company.

Sen. Landreneau: Damn, Dick, I know some of these men, some by name and some by reputation. If I had a list of donors like this, I might consider making a run for president. But a question, Mr. Perryman: I have read in Harper's and various other well-regarded publications that Indian Territory is rife with scoundrels cheating, stealing, even killing innocent Indians for their allotted lands. How will your Indian stockholders be protected?

Mr. Perryman: That, Senator, is the aspect of this endeavor that had given me the most pause. A few years ago, I was a member of the Creek police, called the lighthorsemen, engaged in bringing to justice a man who had murdered at least three people for their headrights. Our efforts ended tragically. Both the killer and a lighthorse officer were killed. He was my best friend, Senator.

Sen Landreneau: My sincere condolences, sir. Please go on.

Mr. Perryman: I asked Waite Phillips, of Phillips Petroleum Company, who has created literally dozens of corporations, how to solve this problem and he said American corporate law anticipated such an eventuality and allows for the issuance of a class of stock called "preferred." Preferred stock is called preferred because holders of this class of stock are paid dividends first, before holders of common stock. But preferred stock may not be bought, sold or traded without the consent of the board of directors. It can, however, be passed down to heirs just like any other part of an estate.

Sen Landreneau: Marvelous idea. You got this figured out. Dick, I'm all for this deal.

Sen Pettigrew: I agree, Senator Landreneau. Mr. Perryman, you have hit upon a scheme for the Indian and the white man to meet in the middle, folding the old ways into the new. I will this day inform the Secretary of the Interior that he may release all impounded mineral lease payments being presently held in the name of the Osage tribe. I will further inform him that the transfer of mineral rights from the Osage to the new Indian Territory Illuminating Oil Company is not only within congressional intent, it may well redefine United States and tribal relationships for the coming decades. Well done, Mr. Perryman."

Edward ran to the Western Union office near the Willard Hotel.

"Please send this telegram to James Bigheart, care of the *Herald*, Pawhuska, Indian Territory: 'Prepare a feast, Chief Bigheart. We won. The Osage will not have empty bellies now.'"

Or forever, as it turned out.

EPILOGUE

1900 proved to be a banner year for Benjamin Perryman. His front-page editorial "Defeated by an Army of Clerks"—an elegy to the full-blood Indian, typified by Chitto's quixotic battle against modern bureaucracy—was widely reprinted in newspapers across the country, including the Chicago *Tribune* and Los Angeles *Times*. It also won him the prestigious Indian Territory Press Association Man of the Year award.

On Christmas Day, 1900, Benjamin Perryman and the former Enid Thompson were wed.

That summer Benjamin received a letter from Tom Sixkiller saying that Chitto had made it to the King Ranch and they were riding together again. He heard nothing further until 1905, when Benjamin received an envelope containing an article from the Brownsville *Courier/Post*. It was a eulogy to Tom Sixkiller, entitled "Last of the Lighthorsemen." There was no letter with the clipping, not surprising since Chitto had never learned to read and write. Chitto was never heard from again.

In 1901 Henry Foster and his two brothers struck oil on land just north of the modern day town of Fairfax in Osage County. The Osage Pool proved almost as big as the Glenn Pool near Bartlesville, and in only a few years made Osage tribal members per capita the wealthiest nation in the world. The pool continues to be productive to this day.

Edward Perryman's first dividend check as a stockholder of the Indian Territory Illuminating Oil Company, representing a share of the impounded lease payments, was for $65. His second dividend payment, made in 1905, was for $21,000, more than his father had made in his entire life. Edward spent a good chunk of that payment for two Steinway concert grand pianos. One he donated to the University of Tulsa. The other was for Maud, in their new home in the hills overlooking what is today Southern Hills Country Club.

Edward and Maud began their family with daughter Elizabeth in 1903 and son Jubal in 1906. Martin would come along in 1910.

In 1906 Edward was asked by Tulsa businessmen to head up the Sequoyah State Organizing Committee. Its purpose was to establish the Indian Territory of the Five Civilized Tribes as a state in the Union, separate from the Oklahoma Territory. It was one of Edward's few failures. In November, 1907, Indian Territory ceased to exist and was folded in as the eastern portion of the 46th state, Oklahoma.

Today, the Muscogee/Creek Nation has a tribal police and security force called the lighthorse, with a chief and a staff of 46. It is headquartered in Okmulgee.

THE END

AUTHOR'S NOTE

    Benjamin Perryman was *very* loosely based on a real man, L.C. Perryman, who was a Creek newspaperman and politician. He turned out to be a real scalawag to his own people, as he became chief briefly and robbed the Nation blind, so the comparison stopped there.

    Osage chief James Bigheart was real, as was Creek chief Isparhecher. Chitto Harjo, believe it or not, was real, but I invented his back story. The oilmen are real, too.

    Eeverybody else is fictional. So am I, very often.

AUTHOR'S NOTE

ABOUT THE AUTHOR

Jack Shakely is a fourth-generation Oklahoman of Muscogee/Creek descent.

After a successful career as head of one of the largest philanthropic foundations in California, he returned to his first love of journalism. His novel *Che Guevara's Marijuana and Baseball Savings and Loan* won the prestigious Oklahoma Book Award in 2014. His novel *The Confederate War Bonnet* was awarded the gold medal in two categories, historical fiction and mid-west regional fiction, by the National Independent Publishers' Association in 2009.

Shakely lives in Rancho Mirage, California.